Comments on other *Amazing Stories* from readers & reviewers

"Tightly written volumes filled with lots of wit and humour about famous and infamous Canadians."
Eric Shackleton, *The Globe and Mail*

"The heightened sense of drama and intrigue, combined with a good dose of human interest is what sets Amazing Stories *apart."*
Pamela Klaffke, *Calgary Herald*

"This is popular history as it should be... For this price, buy two and give one to a friend."
Terry Cook, a reader from Ottawa, on **Rebel Women**

"Glasner creates the moment of the explosion itself in graphic detail...she builds detail upon gruesome detail to create a convincingly authentic picture."
Peggy McKinnon, *The Sunday Herald,* on **The Halifax Explosion**

"It was wonderful...I found I could not put it down. I was sorry when it was completed."
Dorothy F. from Manitoba on **Marie-Anne Lagimodière**

"Stories are rich in description, and bristle with a clever, stylish realness."
Mark Weber, *Central Alberta Advisor,* on **Ghost Town Stories II**

"A compelling read. Bertin...has selected only the most intriguing tales, which she narrates with a wealth of detail."
Joyce Glasner, *New Brunswick Reader,* on **Strange Events**

"The resulting book is one readers will want to share with all the women in their lives."
Lynn Martel, *Rocky Mountain Outlook,* on **Women Explorers**

EXTRAORDINARY ACCOUNTS OF NATIVE LIFE ON THE WEST COAST

EXTRAORDINARY ACCOUNTS OF NATIVE LIFE ON THE WEST COAST

Words from Huu-ay-aht Ancestors

NATIVE/HISTORY

by Kathryn Bridge

PUBLISHED BY ALTITUDE PUBLISHING CANADA LTD.
1500 Railway Avenue, Canmore, Alberta T1W 1P6
www.altitudepublishing.com
1-800-957-6888

Extreme care has been taken to ensure that all information presented in
this book is accurate and up to date. Neither the author nor the
publisher can be held responsible for any errors.

Publisher	Stephen Hutchings
Associate Publisher	Kara Turner
Series Editor	Jill Foran
Digital Photo Colouring	Scott Manktelow

We acknowledge the financial support of the Government
of Canada through the Book Publishing Industry Development
Program (BPIDP) for our publishing activities.

Altitude GreenTree Program
Altitude Publishing will plant twice as many trees as were used
in the manufacturing of this product.

National Library of Canada Cataloguing in Publication Data

Bridge, Kathryn Anne, 1955-
Extraordinary accounts of Native life on the West Coast / Kathryn Bridge.

(Amazing stories)
Includes bibliographical references.
ISBN 1-55153-791-5

1. Nootka Indians--Folklore. 2. Nootka mythology. I. Title. II. Series: Amazing
stories (Canmore, Alta.)

E99.N85B75 2004   398.2'08997955   C2004-902100-1

An application for the trademark for Amazing Stories™
has been made and the registered trademark is pending.

Printed and bound in Canada by Friesens
2 4 6 8 9 7 5 3

Contents

Prologue

The earth shook and the sky darkened as clouds obscured the full moon. Trees swayed, their branches brushing against one another. From below was heard a sound that seemed almost primal, a deep, penetrating moan. And then came the silence. An eerie aloneness, a moment that stretched into two, and then three — an emptiness when the comforting sounds of the world ceased and an expectation grew. Where was the breeze? Where was the lapping of the waves on the beach? Where were the geese and the owls in the forest?

And then it began. Beneath it all was movement, a sliding, an inertia and a melting. In a flash the subtleties became reality, the sliding intensified, and the sand melted beneath the houses. The clouds parted and the moonlight revealed a glistening world. Liquid poured from the beach, from the forest floor and the meadow. It mixed with the earth, which was suddenly porous. Everything slid within; the houses sank into the soup without a whimper. Not a voice to be heard.

Silence again, and an overwhelming expectation. Twinkling in the moonlight far from the shore was a wall, 20 metres high and moving steadily towards the land. Behind it was a void, and before it was absence. Within it was a force unimaginable. When it hit the beach the wave did not stop, it climbed over the rocks and the bushes, over the hemlock and fir and cedar trees, snapping them instantly. When the wave drew back it pulled with it all the broken world, stripping the land of everything. The people of Clutus were no more.

Introduction

There is a special place on the west coast of Vancouver Island. It is a combination of rocky cliffs fronting onto the wild Pacific Ocean, of sheltered beaches, bays and estuaries, lakes, mountains, and forests. Geographically, this area is located on the southeastern shores of Barkley Sound, stretching east to Coleman Creek and then southwards along the Pacific coastline towards Clo-oose. Inland, the area encompasses the length of the Sarita and Pachena Rivers and their lakes. The landscape is plentiful and supports a wide variety of plants and animals. The ocean abounds with all manner of plant life, crustaceans, fishes, and sea mammals. Over the millennia, the rivers and streams have supported plentiful runs of salmon. This place is the ancestral home of the Huu-ay-aht First Nation, who have lived there since the beginning of time. This book is their story, written from their perspective, about the creation of their world and the events that have occurred since the beginning, as well as those that took place after the first "outsiders" came to their shores.

The Huu-ay-aht are part of the larger culture of Nuu-chah-nulth speaking peoples of western Vancouver Island. Their world includes relationships with neighbouring First

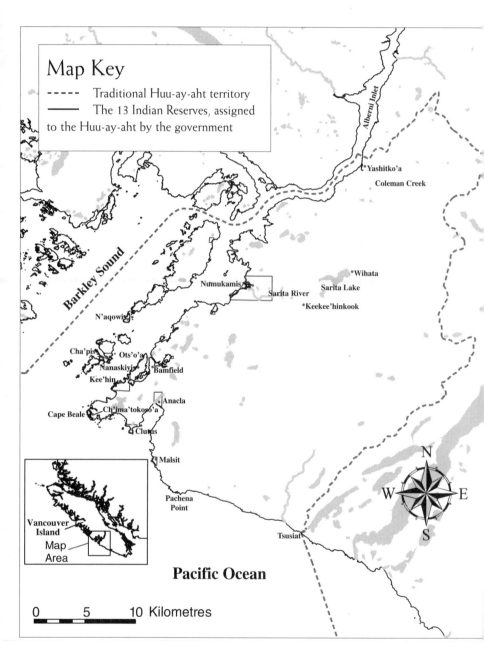

Map Key

- - - - Traditional Huu-ay-aht territory
——— The 13 Indian Reserves, assigned to the Huu-ay-aht by the government

Barkley Sound

Alberni Inlet

Yashitko'a
Coleman Creek

Wihata
Numukamis
Sarita Lake
Sarita River
Keekee'hinkook

N'aqowis

Cha'pis
Ots'o'a
Nanaskiyis
Bamfield
Kee'hin

Anacla
Cape Beale
Ch'ima'tokoso'a
Clutus

Malsit

Pachena
Point

Tsusiat

Vancouver
Island
Map
Area

Pacific Ocean

N
W   E
S

0   5   10 Kilometres

Nations, sharing the abundance of foods found in their territories. Over the centuries they have changed and adapted as both natural and man-made events have presented challenges. For thousands of years, the Huu-ay-aht lived on the land and sea according to age-old traditions and practices. The ocean supplied fish, whales, seals, otters, and shelled creatures. The forests of tall, strong trees provided wood for houses, for carving canoes, and for weaving baskets and rope. The deer and elk, the berries, fruits, and edible plants, provided nourishment. What the Huu-ay-aht could not harvest in their own territory, they purchased, traded, or bartered with other First Nations along the coast and inland.

The arrival of the outsiders, beginning with explorers such as Captain James Cook in 1778, initiated a period that forever changed the world of coastal First Nations. The Nuu-chah-nulth word for these outsiders is mamatni, meaning "those whose houses float about on the water" — an appropriate description for a people who were initially encountered lost in the fog and unaware of where they were.

Today, the Huu-ay-aht remain a strong people, assured of their heritage, protective of their territories and traditions. They live in modern times, yet remain grounded in the knowledge of their own ways. Their history has, until recently, been mostly an oral tradition, passed down through the generations. The Huu-ay-aht did not create books for others to read, but kept their knowledge amongst their own. Times have changed. It is now well past the time when we outsiders should learn more about these First Nations who occupy the land we now call Canada.

The information in this book comes directly from Huu-ay-aht sources. In most cases, the Huu-ay-aht place names and personal names are used, but in some cases, in the interest of clarity for a general audience, the anglicized versions also appear. A glossary of Huu-ay-aht place names is included at the end of the book. I have adapted Huu-ay-aht accounts — about the old times, about their ways of doing things, and about events in the past — from a variety of sources, principally from translations of interviews given by elders to anthropologists and others who sought them out. In some cases I have woven the threads from different versions of stories, and from different speakers, together for a better narrative result.

The foremost source was a chief named Louie Nookmiis (1881–1964). Chief Louie was hereditary chief of the Huu-ay-aht, and his lineage is documented back through the famous Chief Tliishin from Kee'hin. He provided information on Huu-ay-aht culture and history to government officials and anthropologists in the early 20th century, then on through the decades to different linguists, anthropologists, and people interested and respectful of the history. The tape-recorded stories he told to Eugene Arima in 1964, just a few months before his death, provide the basis for many of the chapters presented here. Chief Louie played a significant role in documenting the culture and traditions of his people. He

Introduction

recounted Huu-ay-aht history as he had learned it from his father, and his father's father. His oral accounts of the history include not only that of the last 200 years or so, but encompass truths about ancestors and the Huu-ay-aht world view. Other elders recounted Huu-ay-aht history to interested outsiders as well. Among them were Klamahouse, who, born in 1826, was an elder when Chief Louie was a young boy; Hyna'um (also known as Mr. Bengi), who in 1922 recounted to Alfred Carmichael stories about his youth in the village of Kee'hin; Sa'sawatin and his wife Yima'uk, who collaborated with Hyan'um to provide accounts of the great flood; and William, a Tseshaht man of Huu-ay-aht ancestry who was born in either 1869 or 1870. William's understanding of the history of the Barkley Sound tribes is apparent in the variety of accounts he recounted to anthropologist Edward Sapir in 1913 and 1914.

The Huu-ay-aht Chiefs and Council approved the writing of this book, recognizing that it is intended for a general audience, not for the specialist, and that it is to serve as an introduction to the complex and rich history of these peoples.

Chapter 1
Chief Louie and the Four Great Spirits

Chief Louie Nookmiis looked out on the Land, across the sturdy golden grasses that crept out at the edge of the salal and fir forest, to the cobble beach and the waves that rolled gently against the sloping pebbles. His gaze swept out across the ocean, where deep beneath its surface lay hidden the wealth of plants and creatures that provided food for his people. The sun's fading light cast the waters in a rosy iridescence, while far offshore, a whale breached, spouting water from its blowhole. The unique expiration of water and air could be heard clearly as the sound travelled in the afternoon peacefulness.

"All is one," Chief Louie murmured in response. "All is one." And he turned back to his chair, which stood on the

Chief Louie Nookmiis, on the porch of his house, Bamfield Inlet, 1963.
He is holding some fur sealing spearheads.

lawn in front of Aguilar House at the head of Bamfield Inlet.
He sat for a while, silent and thoughtful, turning inwards in
preparation. Much depended upon his accuracy, his recall,
and his thoroughness. To him was given the responsibility of
knowing the ways of his people and to teach those ways to
others. The younger generation listened to him as he spoke,
but they did not all hear, hear in that special way so necessary

for the history to remain whole, to be transferred from father to son, and to his son, and his son's son.

"We must use what we have," he reminded himself once more, and turned to the anthropologist beside him. "All right, I'm ready. Start the recorder." And Chief Louie Nookmiis, hereditary chief of the Huu-ay-aht people, began to speak.

"Four Great Spirits keep our world," he said, pausing briefly to select his words. "They give shape to all we see and all we are. They are the beginning and the always. They define what we see and together they create the Huu-ay-aht World. These Great Spirits are Land, Above, Horizon, and Undersea.

"The Great Spirit of the Land rules over all the oceans and rivers and mountains, lakes, forests, and beaches. The tiniest drops of clear dew on the grasses, the new soft green needles on the fir trees, the rounded pebbles on the beach, are all small parts of this Great Spirit.

"The stars in the night sky, the moon, the sun, and the warm light in the summer all come from the Great Spirit Above. As does the wind and the rain, soft in summer, but cold and lashing in winter. Rain that fills up the Land — makes our rivers strong and the oceans plentiful. Above controls clouds and storms and the healing sunshine.

"Horizon is the doorway for travellers, ever-changing as we move on the Land. Horizon tells us about what is coming. Look out upon the ocean and see where the world ends. Horizon is the Great Spirit who controls the interfaces. When we look out over the ocean — as far as is possible — we see the beginning of Horizon; when the mountains touch the Sky, and where the Land meets the Sky, when the eye can see no farther, this is Horizon.

"The Great Spirit Undersea directs the oceans and the tides, and its waters provide food for all the creatures of the Land and the Sky. Undersea is powerful — as powerful as the waves that dash the shores and smooth each pebble and rock on the beach. Undersea is mysterious, for it houses life that can only survive in water and in darkness, deep below.

"In the beginning our world was the home for supernatural creatures. The Thunderbird, the Giant Shark, ya'i (the spirits of the mountains), and the pok mis (the wild people of the woods) are just some of these. There were no people the way we are today. The animals also lived in this world, but they were different, they had two selves. The coverings of the animals — their fur, their scales, and their feathers — were like clothing. Whenever the animals took their clothing off they became kuu-us, that is, they became like people. The animals roamed all around the Island and had homes right in their territories. Bears, the elk and the deer, racoons, minks, beaver — all had homes and houses. The birds in the sky all had homes on the land. Whenever they entered their homes, they took their clothing off and suddenly transformed into a kuu-us, such as us, the way we are now.

"Eventually, some of the animals decided they liked to stay as kuu-us, and these ones became our first ancestors.

This was a long time ago. My grandfather told me this is how our people were created."

The anthropologist turned off the tape recorder and both men looked at each other as they rose from their chairs.

"Could we have a short break now?" the anthropologist asked.

"Just for a minute," Chief Louie replied. "I've just barely got started, and I have so much more to relate. Now is the time for me to tell you what I know, what my people know, about who we are and how our world is made."

"All right, I'll just have a quick stretch and let's get back to it."

After a few more minutes, the two settled back. Family members arrived and they, too, settled themselves down in preparation for a good listen. And then Chief Louie picked up the thread of his story.

"All this creation happened at Useless Inlet. It began there, in the shadow of the Thunderbird Mountain, and then gradually spread throughout the land. The birds and deer, bear, mink, elk, and other animals who wanted to remain as animals did so. They put their hides back on and returned to the forest. The others took off their hides, never to replace them. They became human and no longer shared lives with the animals. This was the first separation.

"Much had to be learned to be human. We had to learn to hunt these animals in order to feed ourselves. We had to hunt the animals, and to kill them and to eat. We had new bodies and learned about the differences between women and men. We had to learn how to produce babies, and about the roles of mothers and fathers, and then grandparents, in the upbringing of children. We learned to respect and carefully look after all our resources. We learned to only catch what we needed, to conserve our sea resources and take only the species we needed for food. This was all taught at Useless Inlet and then sent throughout the Land."

Chief Louie then glanced at the faces of those listening. It was to his own family that he now spoke.

"When I was young, I heard about Ko'o'shin. Ko'o'shin is the Raven. This story was told to me by an elder whose name was Klamahouse. This is what he told me. This is from the days when animals and people were not yet separated. The Raven was chief of the village between Bamfield and Sarita on the ocean. When Ko'o'shin was at home he appeared as an ordinary human being. When he travelled, he donned his coat of black feathers. Ko'o'shin had two children, a boy and a girl, but he was widowed and lonely so he resolved to find a new wife. One morning, he put on his coat of black feathers and went outside his house, leaving his children alone. This Raven then flew to many different villages, first to the village of the Ucluelets, then to the village of the Ahousahts, then the Hesquiahts, and then to the Mowachahts, and finally he arrived at a village that lay midway between Nootka and Kyoquot Sounds. He had flown a long distance and was tired. Ko'o'shin lighted on a spruce tree that stood on the bank of a stream near this village. As he rested, a beautiful maiden came out of one of the houses carrying a woven bucket. Behind her raced two young boys who ran down the bank and into the river, where they were instantly transformed into two fish who then leaped and swam about in the water.

"Ko'o'shin called to the maiden, but did not use words. He communicated with the thoughts from his mind. 'Please dip your bucket in the stream under the spruce tree in which I sit, for I am tired and thirsty and would like a drink of cool water.' She understood, and dipped her bucket into the stream. As she lifted the bucket up, however, a sudden thirst came upon her and she dipped her hand into the bucket to scoop some water to drink. When she did this, Ko'o'shin shook the branch of the spruce tree and a few needles fell down over the maiden. As she drank, she swallowed one. It was very sharp and it choked her, so she left the bucket and ran back to the house, coughing and sputtering as she went. The girl's father was chief of the tribe, and when his daughter came choking into the house he was in a panic. She began to spit blood, and then died. The chief and his wife wailed at the loss. It was a great sorrow.

"After a time, they wrapped her body in a blanket, put the body into a cedar box, and tied the box up with a rope of cedar bark. This coffin was then placed in a canoe. The men of the village paddled the canoe across the bay to a point opposite the village. Here they left it. Ko'o'shin watched and flew to the place where the body lay. With his beak he untied the knot on the cedar rope and took the blanket off the face of the dead girl. This Raven had special magic medicine, which he put into her mouth, and the girl began to breathe once more. He spoke to her and said, 'I will marry you and take you to my home.' He then picked her up, for she was very weak, and put her on his back. He cautioned, 'You must keep your eyes closed, for you are not yet strong. We are going home.'

"Ko'o'shin retraced his journey and stopped at each of the villages again, this time to rest. Each time he told the girl to keep her eyes closed. 'If you open your eyes we will fall from the sky. Hold on to me tight, put your arms around my neck and we will fly home.' But really, what Ko'o'shin wanted was that she not know where he was taking her. As they got closer to his village, Ko'o'shin told her a little more about himself, who he was, and about his family and village. The last leg of the journey occurred in darkness because the Raven did not want anyone to see that he had a young maiden with him. Finally he reached his house and found the children very hungry, for they'd had no food while he was away. Ko'o'shin made a fire and everyone went to bed.

"The next morning Ko'o'shin flew to a high tree and watched the coming and going in the village. He saw the canoes come in from fishing and watched as the fish were cleaned. When the people left, he flew down and picked up what scraps he could find. That evening he returned home and took off his black coat. He did not bring food for his wife, who was very hungry. 'Why did you not bring food?' she asked, but received no answer. For the Raven did not understand the hunger of one who is not a Transformer.

"One evening he returned home and found his new wife and the children very happy. They all had been eating. Ko'o'shin smelled the odour of fish and sniffed around trying to find it, but he could not. He then left the house. His wife asked the little girl to pass her dish, which she did. It was filled with water, and when the wife put her little finger into this water, a dog salmon came out of her finger. This was a secret. The little girl was instructed not to tell her father that his new wife could make salmon appear from her finger. But later that evening, Ko'o'shin took his daughter with him to the beach to gather wood. He questioned the girl and she would not tell. Ko'o'shin became very angry and threatened to leave her on a small island that would be submerged at high tide. The child relented and told her father the truth. They returned home and pulled the canoe up on the beach.

"Ko'o'shin then called to his wife. 'Come and swim with me.'

"'Yes,' she replied. 'We will swim tonight. Go to the creek and pile up stones to make a dam so the water will be deeper.'

"Ko'o'shin went out and made four deep pools. That night his wife put her hands in each of the pools, one by one. Each time, dog salmon appeared in the pools. 'Tell all the people to come and take salmon, for there is lots for all.' The people came and took many salmon to smoke for the winter food. Ko'o'shin also took salmon — he took an entire canoe load. He hung them all up to dry and then began to bring in wood for the fire. It took several trips to bring in all the wood. Twice while his arms were filled with wood, his head brushed a salmon, which was hanging up on a drying rack. The second time he became very angry, pulled the salmon off the drying rack and threw it down on the ground. His wife was offended, as she was of the salmon family. All the salmon were insulted and returned to the water again. At the last, his wife too turned into a dog salmon and swam away."

By now Chief Louie's listeners had grown in numbers. They sat on the porch, the four stairs leading to the garden, and the base of the steps. As he talked, they arrived silently and took their places, all eyes trained on his face. These were stories from long ago, stories that had meaning for each one of them. They waited patiently for the next one to begin.

Chapter 2
The Great Flood

I magine what would happen if the rain would not stop and the seas rose, if water covered the land with no escape from wetness, cold, and soaking. Imagine the fierce wind ripping through the trees, lashing the rain into stinging pellets of ice, while thunder boomed all around. Imagine the panic, the sheer terror of a people whose world suddenly turned against them. Add to this a sudden and continuous darkness. No light and great desperation. This was what happened thousands of years ago. It was a global event of such magnitude that stories recounting this flood are meshed in the fabric of cultures around the world.

Oral traditions, art, and written sources worldwide all

record a common cataclysmic event: the great flood, when the rains came and did not cease until the world as was known was covered in water and most living things perished. The Christian biblical account in Genesis features Noah, who built an ark to carry his family and pairs of animals above the floodwaters. When the floodwaters receded, the ark rested on Mount Ararat. In Mesopotamia, god-king Gilgamesh journeyed to speak with Utnapishtim, flood survivor whose great boat brought his family and many living things to safety through seven days and nights of rain and darkness. Utnapishtim's boat rested on the top of Mount Nimish and then the floodwaters receded. Mayan tradition, as recorded in the Popol Vuh, also tells of the great flood, and Nez Perce history states that the people had to climb Mount Yamustus to survive.

Chief Louie tells a story of how one group of Huu-ay-aht ancestors survived this flood. The story is set within Barkley Sound at a place called Mugh-yuu.

"Something was wrong at Mugh-yuu because the tide withdrew from the shore. It was not like an ordinary low tide, or the big tides that come in the spring, but a very curious situation. For several days the tide drew out from the beach. In the morning it drew back, and at night-time it continued to draw back, exposing more and more sand. Everything was drying up because of the way this low tide exposed the sea creatures and sea plants. Blennies flopped in ever-shrinking pools of ocean water trapped in rock crevices. The feather-like plumes of sea anemones, which normally graced the tide pools, were now completely out of the water and shrivelled up. The oyster beds died and the little hermit crabs scuttled about looking for moisture.

"Something was very definitely and terribly wrong. You could see gravel for miles as the tide kept going down. The tide went all the way down to the big halibut banks, which were normally well underwater, some 20 kilometres from shore. Without the water, the reefs looked like mountains and stretched out from a huge gravel creek.

"This was a story passed on to the chiefs." Chief Louie reminded his audience. "This is something our people witnessed hundreds and hundreds of years ago. These elders of long ago told the people to prepare, 'For the waters will rise again,' they said. They wanted the people to be ready. 'Pull the great canoes down to the beach and tie them together to make them strong, strong enough that we might place all the cedar boards from our houses, and all our belongings into the canoes.'

"Quickly the people gathered all the cedar ropes that they used for whaling and they lashed the canoes tightly together. All at once a cry went out and faces turned towards the dry ocean bed. A small trickle of water now appeared along the exposed sand and gravel. The tide was starting to flow. The elders' prediction was fast becoming reality. Suddenly everyone was gravely serious as the people realized that they were running out of time. Would the waters come slowly and gently refill the bay, or would the tide come back all in one wave? In that case they had no time to lose.

"Nanolinal was the name of the chief who went into the first canoe. Soon all were seated inside the canoes with all the children, animals, food, and household supplies around them. By the time the darkness came, the canoes began to drift with the strong surge. Up, up the canoes went on the swell of a gigantic ocean roll. Up, up they went, soon pulled far from their homes. Fierce winds stirred the ocean and threatened to capsize the canoes. Luckily for some, they had tied sealskin floats to the canoes. These are the floats the whalers use to keep a whale's carcass afloat. Those with the floats tied to their canoes survived the storm and ocean turmoil and were saved. But many lives were lost as canoes slipped under the ocean.

"Darkness was all around, and soon in the distance, but seeming ever closer, came great booms which echoed in the night. What terrible being could cause such pounding terror? Finally there came a dawn of sorts, for it was still very black all around. The people who had survived looked out from their canoes to see that they were far off from Sarita and drifting now towards an enormous rock jutting up out of the water. This rock was actually the tip of the great mountain called Kaka'apiya. It was a sacred place. Here lived the Thunderbird, which now flapped its wings, creating a great sound of deafening thunder. The mountaintop was afire. Black ash and rocks spouted in all directions. The great

A dead whale awaiting slaughter at Cha'pis, Diana Island, circa 1910.

Sea Serpent was swinging its tail around, hitting the sides of the mountain, causing fire and devastation. No wonder the sky was dark.

"The canoes stayed clear of the Thunderbird and the Sea Serpent. As the fires died down, the Thunderbird ceased its flapping. The people found an outcropping on the rock and tied the canoes to it. Then the water grew still and the wind ceased. Into this silence came a sucking sound, the sound of the tide pulling back. It was so strong that many of the ropes on the canoes snapped like threads. Canoes sank or got caught by the strong current. But a lucky few survived and were able to guide their canoes down with the water. As the water receded, the clouds lifted and the sun appeared. Looking out around them, the people could see extraordinary distances and realized that little had survived this cataclysmic flood.

"A few months later, as they re-established themselves on the land, the people started finding many of the canoes that had sunk, and they travelled great distances looking for survivors. This is how they learned that tribes such as the Nitinat and the Namintath had also found refuge, and that when the tide had risen to its fullest, it had reached inland all the way to Sproat Lake, and it was there that canoes from many nations had anchored.

"The land changed greatly from this disaster, and it took time for nature to right itself. Never since has the world experienced such a thing, and hopefully, never again."

The Elderberry Root

In 1922, an Huu-ay-aht elder by the name of Hyna'um (also known as Mr Bengi), recounted a story of the great flood as it had been told to him by his uncle, Cheepsaw, brother of Tsa'tsa'wist'a. Hyna'um's narration was captured on paper by visitor Alfred Carmichael, who was camping with his family on Brady's Beach, just outside Bamfield. (Carmichael heard several of Hyna'um's Huu-ay-aht stories that summer. Theirs was a fortunate collaboration, for some of Hyna'um's accounts proved to be the only surviving versions of important Huu-ay-aht histories.) The following version adapts the core of Hyna'um's narrative.

"The flood came at a time when the people stretched all along the coast, and when distinctions between the tribes did not exist. One group of people lived in great numbers at Nitinat. These people were whalers and strong in their canoes. They hunted blue whales and humpback whales. The Nitinat chief, whose name was Cha'ut'sem, lived at the mouth of a creek on the south side of Nitinat Lake, and it is here that the story begins.

"One year, when the winter came, the rains began. It was strong rain, forever rain. The ground could hold no more. The water came into the houses, wetting the living areas and making the food mildew from the damp. The people became very afraid. Cha'ut'sem, too, was afraid, especially when the water came right up to his house. So he told his people: 'We must do this. Strip cedar bark to make ropes. Make many ropes and make them long and strong. Make more ropes than you have ever done before, because they are needed. Then load all your goods into your canoes and pack them tightly. Leave space for your children and your parents. Then, when all is ready, tie your ropes together to make them very long. Tie one end to an elderberry root. But listen to me, do not tie them to the spruce root, or the hemlock, or the giant cedar, for their roots do not go deep into the earth.'

"When the people heard this they made noise and talked amongst themselves. The people were very frightened. They did not do as their chief asked. They believed that the mighty trees would be best to hold their canoes, far better than a thin gnarled string of root. So they tied the cedar ropes to the big trees, and the water rose. The rain continued strong, forever rain. Harsh winds blew and the water beneath their canoes boiled and swirled with its power. The spruce, the cedar, and the hemlock roots did not hold to the ground. The trees fell down and broke many of the canoes or else the ropes broke and canoes drifted out to the ocean. Many of the people were killed.

"But Cha'ut'sem, his wife, and his four daughters remained safe in their huge canoe, which was six fathoms long. They were spared, for they had tied strong ropes to the elderberry. Although the rain continued and big winds blew, the elderberry did not pull out of the earth. It held the rope fast and provided a safe anchor for the canoe. After a long while, the water rose very high and covered all the mountains, all except one very high mountain called Kaka'apiya.

"One night, while Cha'ut'sem and his family slept, the canoe floated near to this high mountain and wedged itself into a crook in the rock on the very top of Kaka'apiya. When Cha'ut'sem awoke he saw the Great Spirit sitting in the bow of the canoe. The Great Spirit said to him, 'Do not be afraid. Be of good heart. You and your family will not die. If you sing this song four times, the water will go down.'

"Cha'ut'sem repeated the song four times, and indeed, the water receded, leaving the canoe high and dry on the mountain peak. He waited four days to ensure that the water would not rise again. On the fifth day, Cha'ut'sem and his family returned to their land, but there was no one there. He went to the ocean edge and walked. Some of his people he found at Neah Bay, and some at a place between Sooke and Jordan River. These people were few, but they returned to Nitinat with their chief. They built new houses on the oceanfront at Nitinat. But it was many years before the people multiplied and again spread throughout the land."

Chapter 3
Deep in the Memory, Proven through Archaeology

Perpendicular cliffs, eroded, undercut, and carved by the waves, rise straight up from the open Pacific Ocean. High above, enormous fir trees grow, bent and resistant to the lashing of the wind and the salt spray of winter storms. On this headland lie the remains of a great fortress. Almost impenetrable salal bush rises three metres high, its thick and twisted limbs tangle and obscure the landscape. Beneath and intertwined with tree roots lie depressions in the forest floor, confirming the location of huge structures. Crumbling earth and stone mounds are the remains of defensive walls. Yes, this was once a great place. But now, steadily and surely, nature reclaims it.

Tucked safely in the lee of this headland is Kee'hin village. It too lies hidden beneath the ever-growing and encroaching salal, elderberry, ferns, and great trees. Kee'hin sits on the southern shore of Barkley Sound, three and a half kilometres southwest of Bamfield, and nine kilometres northeast of Cape Beale, just north of today's popular West Coast Trail and next to the Pacific Rim National Park.

Kee'hin fortress and village is ancient and has a mighty history. Archaeological evidence confirms that Kee'hin dates back 5000 years. This was a time when European farmers banded themselves into clans and tribes and built megalithic stone tombs; urban centres developed in the Indus Valley at Mohenjo-Daro and Harappa; Mesopotamian civilization on the Tigris and Euphrates Rivers spawned a priestly society with ziggurats built at Ur; the Yellow River in China held the beginnings of the Hsia Dynasty; and in Egypt, the first of the Great Pyramids at Giza were constructed. Here, at Kee'hin, Huu-ay-aht people also built, but the material they used was wood. In the wet, damp climate of the north Pacific, such material quickly rots. Most of the evidence of the Huu-ay-aht culture — the cedar houses, the carved and ceremonial objects — has not survived through time.

Nevertheless, archaeological research undertaken in recent generations provides hard evidence of human occupation. Barkley Sound has been measured and analyzed. Within Huu-ay-aht territory alone, over 40 village sites are known, in addition to well over 100 camps, used over the

An artist's rendering of what the central village and fortress
of Kee'hin must have looked like. (Illustration by Lori Graves.)

centuries for resource harvesting and as lookouts. Six villages
had defensive sites like Kee'hin. In the sheltered intertidal
areas lie the remains of fish traps made of stone, and canoe
runs in the beach areas. The forest also preserves the telltale
signs of its use. Cedar, the tree most utilized for its bark and
its wood, was harvested throughout the region. The living
trees show signs of bark stripping, and felled trees — chopped
and shaped — confirm widespread wood utilization.

Walking through the Kee'hin site today is not easy, for
the forest has taken control, and all is thick with damp and

greenery. Even so, the depressions marking large communal houses, which held extended families of 30 or more people, are still visible. Fallen timbers now act as nurse logs for the bushes, fir, hemlock, and cedar trees that have encroached on the village site. Behind the village is a hillside lush with gigantic liquorice ferns. At the western edge, scrambling up and over an ancient midden and a tangle of salmonberry bushes, lies the route to the headland and the fortress upon it. It is a forbidding and hidden climb — intentionally so, for village security was crucial.

At its peak, the population of Kee'hin probably reached 500. As the centuries came and went, as war, famine, and shifts in the seasonal rounds for resource gathering changed, the population of Kee'hin fluctuated. Depending upon the time of year, the village could be a busy place. Because of its proximity to the open ocean, Kee'hin in the summer absorbed extra people who came to the outer shore of the Sound to hunt whales and seals. The great red cedar trees in the forests behind the village were considered some of the best for making canoes, and during the winter months, men worked at shaping war canoes, whaling canoes, and other smaller canoes.

Kee'hin, as the centre of Huu-ay-aht culture, was the largest of the villages, and among the oldest. Here, generations of chiefs were born; these were the head chiefs of the tribe. Their exploits are preserved in Huu-ay-aht song and stories. The title of chief was (and still is) inherited through the male line, from father to eldest son. The honorific name for head chief changed through the life of the chief. As a young chief he may have been known as Nanolinal, and as he aged and organized his territorial rights, he became Tliishin. Many of the accounts of Huu-ay-aht history refer to Chief Tliishin, who was, undoubtedly, not always the same man.

In the centuries before contact with the outsiders, Kee'hin was the focus of power in south-eastern Barkley Sound. And when the outsiders arrived, it was successive Chief Tliishins who welcomed these visitors into Huu-ay-aht territory. But by the end of the 19th century, Kee'hin was abandoned because outside economic influences drew the people away. They did not move far, just across the water to Cha'pis, at Dodgers Cove, Diana Island.

Photographs of Kee'hin village taken in the early 20th century show how the forest had already begun to take it over. Only the uprights and ridgepoles of one house frame remain, but outside the house frame stand two six-metre high "welcome figures" carved of cedar. Proud and weathered, these figures represent the first kuu-as, or Huu-ay-aht people, who came from the Sky spirit. The male figure's arms are outstretched in peace, one hand gestures the visitor to come, while a pointed finger on the other hand reminds the visitor to respect Huu-ay-aht laws. The female figure originally carried a cylinder in her hands, which represents the topati, or inherited rights of the chief.

With a little imagination, and the knowledge of past

39

Cedar welcome figures representing Huu-ay-aht "first ancestors"
at Kee'hin village, ca. 1910.

events, it is easy to visualize massive cedar plank houses —
10 or so in number, measuring variously from 10 by 15 metres
in floor size to 25 by12 metres, and rising to 4 metres in height
— set along the platform above the broad and curving beach.
Upon this beach, dozens of whaling canoes and smaller
canoes are drawn up to the high water through a series of
channels cleared amid the stones and gravel to make canoe-
runs. Smoke from the village fires swirls at the interface of the
cleared bush and forest. Dogs bark, children cry out, voices

mix with the regular draw of the waves along the shingle and sand of the beach, in and out, in and out.

Over the centuries, this unique geography — the headland that provides excellent visibility out to the ocean and the entrance to Barkley Sound, across to the Deer Group of Islands, and up Trevor Channel, along with its protected village on the leeward side — led to conflicts between the Huuay-aht and other First Nations who coveted the spot. Many wars were fought and lives lost in its defence. Invaders inevitably came by ocean, so watchmen stationed on the headland had an important responsibility.

But the significance of Kee'hin runs deeper than this recent past. Many of the early accounts, of the time when Huu-ay-aht ancestors still moved between the animal and human worlds, happened at Kee'hin. The escapades of hero adventurers such as Eut'le'ten, a boy with magical powers who was born from tears, all connect with this place. Through the generations, elders told these stories to the young people, who then passed them on to their children. For outsiders, some themes remind us of stories we were told as children. Might common heroic stories, told across cultures and continents, signal a shared past?

The legend of a wild woman of the woods is known in variation among different Vancouver Island First Nations. Her visage is recreated in oversized carved and painted cedar masks, worn by dancers who move and twirl around the fire centred in the traditional big house. In this flickering firelight she is a frightening sight. The following Huu-ay-aht story is but one chapter in a series of supernatural adventures involving the hero Eut'le'ten — the boy who slays the wild woman.

The Wild Woman of the Woods

Danger lurked deep in the forest. Mothers cautioned their children not to tarry when they collected firewood, and to stay together, for a wild woman lived in the forest. Her name was E'ish'so'oolth. She was so tall that when she walked through the forest her head brushed the lower branches of the great fir trees. E'ish'so'oolth was a cheeha — a supernatural creature. Her lodge was hidden far inside the dark and canopied forest. It was made of cedar logs larger than anyone had ever seen before. E'ish'so'oolth would wait patiently, watching. Any girls and boys who wandered too far from their homes might come across this evil cheeha, who would then capture them and take them to her lodge. And there, at her leisure, the children would be eaten — for the cheeha was a cannibal.

E'ish'so'oolth was married to a giant cheeha. He was even taller, and towered over his wife. His strength was greater than that of any man living on the coast. He was a brute, with long matted hair that fell in tangles down around his great shoulders. His scowling face was filthy, and his eyes — eyes that were sunken deep in his skull — glared out, sullen and angry. This cheeha was not a being to trifle with.

He could crush the life out of anything that displeased him.

Whenever people went missing, the Huu-ay-aht said that perhaps they had been captured by E'ish'so'oolth or her husband and taken to their lodge to be devoured at leisure. Naughty children were admonished to behave. "Be good or I will call E'ish'so'oolth!"

One day, some children from Kee'hin paddled a canoe out from their home and landed on a nearby shore, where they planned to gather seaweed. As they set out along the beach, each carried a woven cedar bark container. Soon, one of the younger children became cold and tired, and he cried out to be taken home. The chores were not yet complete, so the others asked the boy to be patient, because they would leave for home shortly. But this child was not to be comforted and again he cried out. The others began to scold him and threatened to call E'ish'so'oolth. The threat had no effect, and the child continued to cry. In jest, one child made the mistake of teasing and called, "E'ish'so'oolth, E'ish'so'oolth, oh come E'ish'so'oolth."

The next moment a terrible being — tall and gaunt with stooping shoulders — stalked out from the forest. It was the cheeha. She carried a mighty walking stick made of a gnarled tree branch. Waving this knotty stick in the air, she cried out, "Who called me by name?"

The children screamed and tried to run away, but as they scattered she laughed fiendishly, stretched out her walking stick, and tripped them as they ran. The cheeha then calmly caught them one by one with her lean hands. Using the sticky pitch from the fir tree, she sealed their eyes shut so that they would not be able to see which way they were going. She then threw the children into a basket on her back and started for home along a hidden track through the forest. But E'ish'so'oolth had to bend each time the path curved under the low and spreading branches of the fir trees, for she was so tall, and the basket on her back was now heavy. As she bent to go beneath these branches, four little hands popped up out of the basket top. Then, when a fir branch brushed the basket top, these little hands grabbed the branch tightly and held on fast. The cheeha kept on going and did not miss the weight of just two children.

With their hearts thumping in their chests, the two children stayed as still as they could until they were certain E'ish'so'oolth had passed. They climbed down the tree limb and together they tried to free their eyes of the pitch. Once they could see a little bit, they ran for the beach, got in the canoe, and headed for home. These lucky children told their mothers the terrible tale of how their playmates were scooped up and taken away. "By now surely they must be at the cheeha's lodge, perhaps they are already eaten," the children said.

Then came a sound as ancient as grief itself. Heartbreaking wails echoed through the village. Parents and grandparents, brothers and sisters, all mourned for the kidnapped children. The mothers sat, arms clasped around their knees, rocking back and forth. Steadily the power of their grief unleashed. They began singing the death lament. For these mothers there was no hope. No one had ever escaped from E'ish'so'oolth. Their children were gone and there was absolutely no way to save them from their fate. For four days and nights the dismal song was heard. Weeks passed by and still they mourned. After a time, though, the healing began, and all but one mother drew comfort. She sat all alone, and each day at dawn, squatted on the sea grass along the shore, chanting the mourning song.

Early one morning, as she sat and cried, her tears flowed down and formed a little pool. This little pool of tears lay balanced among the grass blades. She did not notice it until, out of the corner of her eye, she caught a movement in the sand. The pool of tears was changing into something alive, something that — although very tiny — moved and wiggled. The mother picked up a mussel shell so that she could cradle the tiny form within it.

"What could this being be?" she wondered.

Gently she stood. Cupped in her hands lay the mussel shell with its precious occupant. She carried it into her lodge and set it down in a safe and quiet place. The next day, within the shell lay a wonderful and tiny child. This child grew every day. The woman had to find larger and larger shells — oyster, mussel, and clamshells — to form a cradle. She called this tiny being Eut'le'ten. He grew into a beautiful young boy. His limbs were well formed, his skin fair, and his eyes clear and bright. This child was also wise beyond his years. For him, the most sorrowful thing was to hear his mother weeping, as she continued to do. Her constant pain gave him great sorrow and one day he asked her, "Why do you weep so? Why do you chant the death lament?"

His mother looked at him with love in her eyes, yet sadness in her heart, and she told him about his sister and the tragedy that had befallen her. "E'ish'so'oolth came and took your sister, took her deep into the dark forest. I have no idea if she is alive or dead, I cannot live for the uncertainty and the pain."

" Do not weep, Mother. I will seek your daughter, who is my sister, and I will save her. Show me where she was last seen, and I shall search and find her."

Knowing that Eut'le'ten was a spirit-child and could come to no harm, the woman gave him her blessing. But first she cautioned, "It is best to speak with the two children who escaped. Have them show you where your sister was taken from."

Armed with the children's information, Eut'le'ten started out. When he arrived at the spot described by the two children, he broke through the dense salal that fringed the forest edge. He ducked into the thick woods, around the silvery spruce and the hemlock. As he followed the path, Eut'le'ten learned about the forest, for he was a newly born spirit-child, and although invested with powers, had little knowledge of this place. He learned about salmonberry thorns and devil's club, about mud and swamp, and about the difficulties of travelling in the bush. He saw black bears and other forest creatures, and heard new and different birds.

The trail led him far inland. He travelled a great distance before he came upon a cool stream from which he quenched his thirst. As he stood alongside the water, Eut'le'ten saw the path broaden, and he carefully moved forward. There, in the clearing, was a lodge of such a size that he was dumbfounded. Surely this was the house of E'ish'so'oolth and her husband. But it was dusk, and he debated what to do. Perhaps it would best to wait until morning. If he rested, in the morning he could confront the cheeha in the light. So Eut'le'ten climbed a tree that stood alongside the creek and went to sleep, drawing strength from the forest spirits. He prayed for courage and wisdom and strength to kill the cheeha.

The next morning he awoke to sounds beneath him. Eut'le'ten looked down and saw E'ish'so'oolth coming to wash in the stream. She was a fierce and ugly creature. Carefully he hid in the branches, confident she could not see him. But he was mistaken. As she leaned over an eddy in the stream to bathe, the water reflected the sky and trees, and he too was mirrored. In a flash she turned her eyes upward into the branches and saw Eut'le'ten partly concealed by the foliage. She smiled at him with a triumphant and expectant look, thinking what good fortune she had. Here was another child to capture.

She greeted him. "Good morning young friend, what

brings you so far from your village? You must be cold and hungry. Why not come down from that tree and we can go to my lodge? It is nice and warm inside, for the fire is lit. I have some fresh berries which you are welcome to eat." Eut'le'ten wavered and did not answer right away, so she added, "I can hardly make you out you are so well hidden in that tree, come down so I can see you."

Confident that no harm could befall him, Eut'le'ten scampered down from the tree. E'ish'so'oolth looked at him and realized he was a truly beautiful child. He was perfect. Never before had she seen such a child.

"Why is your skin so fair?" she asked him.

Eut'le'ten answered, "When I was a boy my mother laid me upon the ground with my head on a stone. Then my father placed a large rock on my forehead. This gave me the gift of fairness."

The cheeha was very taken with the beauty of the young boy, and she thought about his words. "Would this work for me?" she wondered. "How much easier it would be to entice young children to my lodge if I was pleasant to look at. The children would not be so afraid if I was fairer."

Eut'le'ten read her mind, and before she had a chance to ask this selfish question herself, he answered it for her. "Would you like me to give you the gift of fairness?" he inquired. "Lie down on the stone here beside the creek. And then if you recline your head, I can place on your forehead a magic stone which will mould your features and make your skin fair."

E'ish'so'oolth determined to try at once, and immediately stretched herself out on her back upon the flat rock. Then Eut'le'ten lifted a great rock and hurled it onto her head. He shouted, "Die E'ish'so'oolth, die! Never again will you steal children!"

But Eut'le'ten was not yet finished his task. The small boy then set out to search for E'ish'so'oolth's husband. It was not too difficult to locate this beast because loud pounding noises gave away his location. Eut'le'ten found the cheeha at work splitting a fallen tree, using wedges formed from the western yew, the hardest of woods. With mighty blows of his stone hammer, he sunk a wedge deep into the log, splitting it open. This cheeha was enormous and ugly. Although Eut'le'ten was prepared, he took a moment to gather his courage and watched as the huge man worked. Thunderous blow after blow fell upon the wedge, sinking it deeper into the log. The cheeha's aim was true. The split grew wider and the sides of the rent pressed upon the wedge, so hard that if the wedge were dealt a glancing blow, it would fly out. As he hammered, the cheeha saw a furtive move out of the corner of his eye. He could feel someone watching him, someone who hid in the bushes.

"No one has any business spying on me," he thought. The cheeha grew angry, but he managed to control himself. "It would be easier to kill this intruder by coaxing him to me than by frightening him off and chasing."

Cautiously, Eut'le'ten approached the cheeha, moving

slowly but deliberately so the giant would not realize that he was frightened. But that only angered the cheeha, who expected fear from everyone who encountered him. The two looked long and hard at each other. The cheeha conceived a plan. Taking his stone hammer, he struck another blow, pretending to hit the wedge then letting the hammer drop deep in the crack and out of reach.

"Come here boy, I need your help. I have lost my hammer within this mighty tree. I cannot reach it, but you are smaller. Please jump in and get it for me as I need it back."

The boy climbed up on the great log and then dropped down into the split, just as the cheeha had requested. The cheeha gave the wedge a sudden tap and it shot out. With a mighty snap, the sides of the great log came together like the mouth of a sea monster.

"Ha, ha!" cried the cheeha, confident that he had killed Eut'le'ten in a single motion. But suddenly, he saw a remarkable thing on the ground before him. A little pool of water formed, and from it there came an unearthly sound. As the cheeha watched, the water moved and took shape, and the boy rose up. Nothing could harm this boy who could change his shape when in danger. He could transform into a primal pool of tears, and then back again into his human shape. Astonished but resourceful, the cheeha covered up for his actions.

"Oh, young boy," he said, "what a miracle. I thought for a moment that you had been crushed within the log. It was my mistake, and what a dreadful mistake it was. But how, tell me how, did you survive this accident? I saw with my own eyes that the log closed tight around you. And then in the next second you disappeared ... and then ... from a puddle of water you reappeared. Tell me, how did you gain this super-natural power?"

"It is a power that can be shared," claimed Eut'le'ten. "Come, I will teach you the way. If we try it just once, you will learn how to transform as well."

The cheeha, like his wife, was weakened by selfishness. He wanted this power for himself. Quickly he reset the yew wedge deep into the heart of the log, opening up a split large enough for him to squeeze into. He carefully slid into the space. It was tight, tighter than he had envisioned.

"Are you ready?" called the boy.

"Yes!" roared the cheeha, shaking the trees with his enthusiasm.

"Then die!" responded Eut'le'ten, and he took the ham-mer up and struck the side of the yew wedge. Out sprung the wedge and the sides snapped together, crushing the cheeha, who shouted wildly in pain. Eut'le'ten ignored the cheeha, whose bones were soon crushed to powder.

Eut'le'ten sped off to the great lodge and entered into it. It was gloomy because the light only entered through the door-way and the smoke-hole. For some time Eut'le'ten was unable to see anything, but gradually his eyes adjusted to the greyness and he made out the shapes of the baskets and other objects in the lodge. In the centre of the room was a smouldering fire, and in the hot ashes lay some heated stones. Beside the fire was a wooden box filled with water, ready to receive the heated stones, which would boil the water. Eut'le'ten's heart was heavy. He moaned. Was he too late to save the children? Had they already met their fate? Then he heard a sound that seemed to come from the far side of the lodge. Turning around, he saw some children imprisoned in basketry.

"Be brave, children," he said. "I am here to rescue you and return you to your homes. My name is Eut'le'ten and I am from your village. E'ish'so'oolth and her husband are both dead, so you have nothing to fear. There is no more danger."

But the children remained frightened. His voice was not familiar to them, and for all they knew, it could be a trick. Eut'le'ten then realized what part of the problem was. The children could not see. Speaking softly, he took a little whale grease and gently wiped their eyelids to remove the pitch that E'ish'so'oolth had used to close them so long ago. Able to see, the children's confidence increased. They looked into Eut'le'ten's eyes and saw that he spoke the truth.

"The cheeha is really dead?" they asked him.

"Yes, and her husband too. Let's go home now."

Out of the lodge they ran, away from the dark and into the sunlit woods, along the path, and eventually out into the bay. There was much rejoicing when Eut'le'ten returned with the children. Gently he led his sister to his mother, and the two were reunited. Now his mother wept with tears of joy.

Chapter 4
West Coast Peoples

The Nuu-chah-nulth First Nations on the West Coast lived in local groups that were part of tribes. Although their language had a common base, dialect and words varied from tribe to tribe. Thus the Huu-ay-aht tribe in Barkley Sound pronounced certain words or phrases differently than the Mowachaht in Nootka Sound or the Ahousaht in Clayoquot Sound. The Huu-ay-aht shared Barkley Sound with other tribes, including the Toquaht, the Tseshaht, the Ucluelet, the Uchucklesaht, and the Hupacasath. Each tribe with its local groups claimed territories. Rights to harvest specific foods from both the ocean and the land were fixed to specific geographical areas, and these areas, or hahoothlees, were owned by individuals within each local group. These hahoothlees have been handed down in families through the generations and are acknowledged and known today. Likewise, the position of chief is hereditary and passes through the male line, from father to eldest son.

Within the Huu-ay-aht tribe, four local groups emerged over its history as long-lived. These groups were basically independent of each other, but had close ceremonial and military relationships. Each local group claimed a different geographical area within southeastern Barkley Sound. These groups were the Huu-ay-aht, the Kee'hinath, the Ch'ima'tokoso'ath, and the Anacla'ath.

In the days before the outsiders came, the tribes in Barkley Sound jostled for rights to territories and resources. Tribes whose villages lay amidst the rocky shores of the outside edges of the Sound had to negotiate with other tribes to obtain a share in accessing their rich salmon rivers. Those rivers especially coveted were the Somass River at the head of the Inlet, the Sarita River on the southern shores of the Sound, and the Henderson and Namint Rivers on the northern shores. All species of salmon were eaten by coastal peoples, but for those who lived on the outside of the Sound, access to the dog salmon was especially necessary — when smoked, dog salmon keeps longest without spoiling.

Those tribes living on the inside areas of the Sound and with access to salmon streams then negotiated with those on the outside edges for the rights to hunt sea mammals on the open ocean, and for drift whale rights. Drift whales are whale carcasses that float along in the tide, eventually beaching or sinking. They represented a relatively easy way to gain the meat and oil of the whale, but the opportunities for whales to drift past the outside tribes to the inside tribes were relatively slim, hence the need for negotiations.

Conflict

Seldom are people satisfied with what they hold, often coveting what is a neighbour's right. In the absence of rights, or of the ability to make alliances, was the option to take by force a strategic or resource-rich area. For the Nuu-chah-nulth First Nations, the balance of power shifted depending upon the strengths of particular tribes and upon the success of alliances and marriages. So politics in Barkley Sound were rarely stable, and warfare was often inevitable.

At times, because of illness, scarcity of food, or calamity, one local group would be weakened, and would have to make an alliance with another group for survival. Some tribes grew strong and thrived, developing aspirations to extend their territories, to claim salmon spawning rivers, herring bays, or defensive sites. War was one way to do this. Intermarriage between local groups, and at times between tribes, was another way that authority and jurisdiction over land shifted as alliances formed. Marriages between high-ranking individuals mingled the blood of both tribes. Affiliations and families thus mixed.

But sometimes events conspired to try the alliances confirmed through marriages. One of the outside alliances made by the Huu-ay-aht was with a people to the south, people who lived at Clallam Bay on the southern shores of the Strait of Juan de Fuca, on the Olympic Peninsula, in what is now the United States. These Clallam people (unlike their Makah neighbours) were not Nuu-chah-nulth speaking peoples, but were Coast Salish, with distinct language and customs. Despite these differences, the Clallam and the Huu-ay-aht forged economic and political links through arranged marriages as a means of attaining security and good connections.

However, as in marriage, harmony is not always possible. Sometimes blame is cast for things done or not done, for insults, for slights intended or not intended. The Huu-ay-aht relations with the Clallam could be stormy. The following story recounts a devastating act of retribution taken against the Huu-ay-aht for perceived or actual wrongs done to Clallam or Clallam-descended people within the Huu-ay-aht community. Chief Louie, who presented this information within the context of two separate stories, estimated that the events occurred about 200 years earlier, some four generations previous.

Further details of the actual assault on Kee'hin came from another source. In 1922, three Huu-ay-aht elders — Sa'sawatin, his wife Yima'uk, and Hyna'um — sat on a sunny beach at Dodgers Cove. Alfred Carmichael paddled over from

Huu-ay-aht elders Sa'sawatin and his wife Yima'uk

his campsite on Brady's Beach to meet them, for he had asked them to talk about the old days at Kee'hin. Hyna'um had lived at Kee'hin as a young boy. Carmichael brought a rough sketch map he had made of the remaining house frames in the village, and Hyna'um told him the names of the heads of each family who had lived in the houses.

Carmichael left an important description of this day and how the elders spoke with him. There was no tape recorder, but the mood of the afternoon is captured in his words: "Old Sa'sawatin started the narrative, then Hyna'um would follow, and old Yima'uk would nod her head approvingly and say 'Ach, Ach, Yes, Yes,' and perhaps chip in with a bit of information … and in the telling their faces lighted up with eagerness. For hours they talked and I questioned."

The Clallam and Nitinat Combine Forces

Tliishin was chief of the Huu-ay-aht, and an extremely powerful man. He lived in the largest house at Kee'hin. At the time of the war, his hahoothlee — the rights and privileges he commanded over the territory — extended over a huge area. According to Chief Louie, Tliishin's hahoothlee stretched from the waterfall at Tsusiat River on the coast east of Cape Beale, all the way to Yashitko'a (Coleman Creek) on lower Alberni Canal. It was a vast territory.

This chief was married to a Clallam woman. It is not recorded if Tliishin had a voice in the choice of his marriage partner, but it is more likely that as a high-ranking person, it was his duty to strengthen his people through an alliance with another tribe. By allying with the Clallam, Tliishin was doing his chiefly duty.

The couple had twin daughters and two sons. It was the second son who caused the troubles. His name was Nasismis, which means "Carrying-Day-on-Beach." He was short-tempered and always fighting. He provoked others and behaved badly towards the women. In games of chance he cheated, and in games of strength he broke the rules. He was very devious. As a second son, he also was jealous of his older brother.

One day, Nasismis killed his older brother — he cut off his head in the way of the Clallam warriors, and then hid the body. Upon returning to his village, Nasismis claimed he was puzzled.

"It was the strangest thing," he told his father. "My brother travelled with me, but then, as I faced out towards the ocean watching the gulls circling at something floating in the water beyond the point, I turned to make some comment, but he was not there. I just saw the last of him as he strode into the forest. I assumed he was trailing a deer and that he would soon return. I was patient, but there came no sight of him. I awaited as the sun came close to the horizon, and then went to the spot where I last saw him. I called, and waited some more, but he did not return."

The story did not sit well with the young men of the village who did not like Nasismis, knowing him to be a liar. The next day they set forth with Nasismis, who showed them where he had last seen his elder brother. Indeed, nothing was to be found and there were no clues. But still the young men persevered and searched at the opposite beach. After a time, the body was discovered. Nasismis was blamed for the murder.

The young men spoke together, for they were very worried. With the eldest son dead, this wicked younger son was next in line to become their chief. It was not right that a man who would someday have much authority could kill his own brother; this was a frightening situation. The young men therefore resolved that they had no choice: they would have to kill Nasismis to prevent future troubles. And so as a group, the young men took Nasismis to a beach and killed him. It was a dangerously bold move to kill a future chief. But in their view there was no alternative. The consequences of this action, however, would prove devastating to the Huu-ay-aht people.

The mother of Nasismis was heartbroken, for she had lost both her sons. She was not convinced that the eldest son had died at the hands of his brother. She blamed both murders on the young men of the village. As soon as she was able, she went home to Clallam Bay, home to tell her people of the deaths. In the spring she returned.

Six months later, in August, word came to the Huu-ay-aht that their southern neighbours, the Nitinat, were planning war on them, and that these Nitinat people had asked the Clallam, Port Angeles, and Lapush peoples to join them. The Huu-ay-aht prepared for war. Each day, the men washed themselves in the cold ocean water and scrubbed their bodies with hemlock until the blood flowed — this made them strong.

Under the cover of darkness, a huge raiding party paddled northwards following the western coastline of the Island to enter Barkley Sound. The raiding party numbered 1500 warriors. It had been a long and dangerous journey for the southern tribes who had joined the Nitinat, for they had come across the Strait of Juan de Fuca, and the open ocean, far from their territory.

But they were motivated. It was an important point of honour for them. They had to take revenge for the deaths of the two brothers who were half Clallam and had been killed by Huu-ay-aht. As sons of a high-ranking Clallam woman, these murdered brothers also had rank. Their murders cancelled out any marriage alliances between these two tribes. The Clallam raiders came to Kee'hin to kill Chief Tliishin, for he alone, as the highest-ranking person, would be sufficient compensation.

Fifty canoes rounded the point from Cape Beale, set to attack three Huu-ay-aht villages, at Ots'o'a, at Nanaskiyis (Brady's Beach), and at Kee'hin. As the warriors approached the promontory at Kee'hin, their paddle strokes became silent, and there was no talk. The warriors had to be cautious. They knew that watchmen generally kept an eye out from behind stone walls high up along the cliff edge, some 30 or so metres above their canoes. But they detected no fires and no movement, only stone walls and silence.

Kee'hin Is Attacked

Safely rounding the fortress rock, the canoes glided in on the waves to the beach on the lee side. It was then that the alarm went out. The invaders had been detected. With fierce battle cries, the Clallam warriors ran up the beach and along the footpaths onto the bench of land where the great houses stood. The fighting began. Stone clubs were swung in the night sky. In the initial confusion, some of the villagers managed to escape from the rear of the houses. These people then ran to a trail behind the fourth house, the house of Chief Tliishin. Up the path they sprinted in a desperate bid to outrace the enemy and reach their fort on the headland.

The chief and his family were amongst those who escaped. As they neared the top of the path, each had to duck beneath a great, heavy log placed across the trail. This was just one of several obstacles set in readiness, for at the last moment, as the invaders crested the trail, the log would be released to roll and smash down upon them. The site of the fortress had been chosen well, for it was impregnable from the ocean side, and only accessible from one route. At the top, the villagers hid behind metre-high defensive walls of earth and stone. From this protected vantage, they threw rocks from a stockpile down upon their assailants.

The fortress included small lodges as additional protection. One lodge also hid an escape route. It was into this lodge that Chief Tliishin and his family members fled. Inside, it was adrenaline and confusion. The lodge was dark, no fire burned. Babies cried and young children hid their heads under their mothers' arms. The young men bristled at being cooped up inside, away from the action. But they were responsible for Tliishin's safety. Far in the back, in the darkest corner of the lodge, panicky hands hurried to move the cedar cooking vessels, the feast bowls, and the cooking utensils. Beneath these was a large flat cedar slab. Scrabbling with fingers, they pried up the slab to reveal a hole that led down through the dirt, to a crevice in the rock below. By wiggling, a full-grown adult could fit through this crevice into a shaft, which opened up into a cave. The cave was underground but above the sea level — a perfect hiding spot, but a spot that could shelter only a small portion of Tliishin's extended family. As quickly as they could, Tliishin and many of the youngest family members squeezed down the hole. Those remaining in the lodge replaced the cedar plank and the cooking vessels. They then prepared to hold off the enemy.

Even those who managed their way up the trail to the fortress never stood much of a chance. By their sheer numbers, the Clallam overpowered the Huu-ay-aht and were victorious. After four days, the battle sounds and the cries of the wounded were heard no more by those hidden deep in the rock of Kee'hin. But Tliishin and the young men and women remained in the cave, not daring to venture forth. Finally the Clallam departed. Although Chief Tliishin had escaped, the Clallam were satisfied because in destroying the entire village, the honour of the Clallam mother had been upheld.

Tliishin and the fortunate group of young people emerged from the cave to find their village burned and destroyed, and all their families clubbed to death and beheaded. It was not a good place in which to remain, for they did not know what further plans the Clallam might be formulating. And if not the Clallam, soon their neighbours would hear about the slaughter and come to take over the Huu-ay-aht territory.

Hidden in the brush near the shore, they found a canoe that had escaped Clallam eyes. To preserve their people, the survivors resolved to seek haven from the Clallam and from others who might harm them. They paddled along the shores of Barkley Sound to their salmon-rich main river. This river, later called the Sarita by Spanish outsiders, was to be their refuge. They paddled the canoe up the river, heading deep into the forest and away from the coast. There they would be safe.

The news of Kee'hin's destruction spread quickly. Anticipating further attacks, many of the Huu-ay-aht in the surrounding small villages fled to the larger villages at Ots'o'a and at Nanaskiyis. These villages were more secure because they had defensive sites adjacent to them. There were many people now camped together. But, as at Kee'hin, they were caught unawares by the approaching warriors. The war canoes came silently onto the beach. Those who survived the first wave of attack retreated to the fortresses. Despite valiant defence, the villages were overrun.

In desperation, parents at the two villages put their children and young adults into whaling canoes, and they paddled away to hide. Travelling independently of Tliishin and his group, these youngsters also made their way up Barkley Sound to the Sarita River, which had in the past afforded protection. They travelled silently, ever alert for their enemies. The first group, the Kee'hin survivors, had headed for Keekee'hinkook, on the south branch of the Sarita. The other villagers, who followed within days of the Kee'hin survivors, went a different route; they stayed on the main branch of the river, paddling and pulling the canoes up its entire length until they reached Sarita Lake. From there they paddled to Wihata, a refuge site that would serve them well.

These survivors took many precautions. Through the years they took great care to keep their location a secret, for they were small in number and vulnerable. For 19 years they remained hidden. They multiplied and became strong, anticipating the time when they could return to the coast and reclaim their territories. But neither of the groups knew of the other's existence, so well were they hidden. Each assumed that they were the only survivors, and each of them mourned for the other.

None of their neighbours knew that these Huu-ay-aht had survived, either. All the tribes knew was that Kee'hin, Nanaskiyis, and Ots'o'a all lay in ruins and that their people had disappeared. As the years passed, other First Nations moved into Huu-ay-aht territories, those territories that were once Tliishin's domain. These interlopers took over some of the old village sites, hunted on Huu-ay-aht land, fished in their salmon streams, and took the drift whales in their waters.

At the mouth of the Sarita River, where the land is flat and the beach is wide, Hach'a'ath and Tseshaht people moved in and established a village. They built it on the very land that the Huu-ay-aht used in salmon season, a land they called Numukamis.

It was a chance encounter one day in the forest, high above the river mouth, when Huu-ay-aht hunters from the hidden villages unexpectedly met. One group came upon an elk that was acting suspiciously; it seemed curiously weakened. They shot at the elk with an arrow, and it died. As the hunters squatted around the carcass in preparation to butcher it, they saw that the elk had another wound from an arrow, but not from one of their arrows. This was the reason the elk was weakened. Wondering what the presence of this strange arrow could mean, they suddenly heard conversation in the forest. The conversation was between people they did not recognize, but who spoke their language.

Tentatively they called out, "Who are you?"

The reply came back. "We are Huu-ay-aht people, we have taken refuge in this place.

Who are you?"

It soon became evident that the hunters were facing others that they had assumed to be dead. Each group had hidden themselves so well that they believed they were all alone in the upper Sarita territory. How odd to face those who had been thought long gone. The groups had mourned for each other, and for their Chief Tliishin, but now, with this chance discovery, the mourning could end. The chiefs and elders in each group met for the first time, and there was great rejoicing. For Tliishin, it was a time of special significance. He was now much older, and had worried about the fate of his people, but now clearly, joined together as one, they gained strength in their numbers.

Speaking amongst themselves, the elders resolved to prepare the people to reclaim their territories. Henceforth they planned together. The young men learned the art of war from these elders, who taught them as they once had been taught. It was a time of intense mental and physical preparation.

But meanwhile, as the training continued, another chance discovery set in motion a timeline for the Huu-ay-aht revenge. At the mouth of the Sarita, at the place called Numukamis, the Hach'a'ath and Tseshaht interlopers had a quandary. For several days in a row now, mysterious objects had been floating down the river. Some were discovered at the beach, and some were spotted on the rocks and back eddies at the river mouth. These objects were none other than grass-formed dummies in the shape of fish — the sort used by young men when they practised spearing salmon. Some of the dummies even had spearheads caught in them. With trepidation, the Hach'a'ath villagers picked up the objects and brought them to their elders. What could they mean?

"It is apparent," the elders said, "that unbeknownst to us, people must live upriver. They must be very confident people to have given away their presence by allowing these practice fish to float away." The elders then began to debate. What should their actions be? That night, a man named

Kwaxswiqol, a slave who many years ago had been taken captive from his Huu-ay-aht village, whispered to his wife.

"I must go upriver and see. If there are people living up there, they may be my people, the people who survived the raids. I will go to see if by any chance my chiefs are alive. They will not kill me if they are my chiefs. Don't you tell any of those who live with us in this house. I will return."

He left at high tide that night, paddled upstream, and then poled and dragged the canoe up the river until he reached a beach just below Tl'itsnit. There, panting in the dark, he could smell the smoke from their fires. Frightened, he still continued on, determined to learn whether his kinsmen lived.

Kwaxswiqol called out to the villagers. Those men on the security watch heard him, and understood his words. They took him before the 10 chiefs, some of whom were elders and could recall the old days. They believed his story. Then they questioned him and, upon learning details concerning the village below, resolved to make a pre-emptive strike. The plan was that Kwaxswiqol should return to the village. On the next morning at daybreak, he and his family would climb up and sit on the roof of their house and sing a tse'yka, a sacred song. This would be the signal to attack. With the family up on the roof, they would be safe and away from the battle.

At sunrise, Kwaxswiqol and his family moved to the roof and began to sing. The world seemed very still, until all at once from the forest came the war cries and frightening sounds of the attackers, who came in hard with their stone clubs. In the village of 80 people, there was bloodshed. Soon the Huu-ay-aht warriors gathered the few surviving Hach'a'ath and sent them back to where they had come from. They were sent away to spread the word. The Huu-ay-aht were once again mighty and now reasserted claim to all their territories.

Power Shifts

During their long history, the Huu-ay-aht have had periods when they were weakened and vulnerable to raids from neighbouring tribes, and also times when they were strong in number and could make overtures against their neighbours, or reclaim lands previously taken. One of the more renowned stories is a saga of war and revenge between the Huu-ay-aht and the Ucluelet, who fought for jurisdiction over Barkley Sound during the 18th century.

This war, which became known as "The Long War," lasted many generations. Finally, after years of fighting within Barkley Sound, an Huu-ay-aht chief, whose name was Nanolinal, grew tired. He had witnessed a 10-year-long series of raids between his people and the Ucluelet and Hach'a'ath. All that had been accomplished were the deaths of many young men, which meant that it was harder for those remaining to hunt for food and survive each year. But still the raids continued, and Nanolinal believed that unless there was a way to end the battles for once and always, all that would be accomplished would be the continued weakening of his people.

"Why are we doing this?" he asked his people. "Why are we fighting all the time? At times many of us are killed. They killed my father. Our country is always in danger. We should work out some way in our method of fighting so that we may kill our enemy once and for all, and get back to a peaceful time." But no one had any idea how they could do this. No one, that is, except Nanolinal. He had a bold scheme.

"Let us go to Sarita River," he said to the people. So 50 young men went to the Sarita River, and there they killed an elk. They killed the elk for its skin to make coats and hats. Then they killed a black bear. They lined the coats and hats with bear bones. Soon they were all equipped with elk-skin coats and elk-skin hats lined with black bear bones. The purpose, of course, was so that spears and arrows would not penetrate them, and their heads would not be broken if hit with a war club. It took three months for all these preparations, which included fasting. Nanolinal believed that overeating made the people weak, so they learned not to eat so much, as a preparation for war.

In July they were ready, and went on a war raid. They wore masks and their elk clothing. Fifty warriors paddled away in canoes, with each canoe holding up to twelve men. They travelled swiftly, with the element of surprise, to Effingham Inlet, home of the Hach'a'ath. Leaving the canoes on the beach, the warriors approached the village through the trees. They emerged from the forest, clubbing and killing. They set fire to the villages and achieved almost total destruction. Not a single Huu-ay-aht warrior was killed or injured. The raid was a total success, due almost entirely to the protective armour, which had given the Huu-ay-aht great confidence. The victors set off for home, returning to Sarita, where they settled.

Soon, news of their prowess spread, and the Huu-ay-aht grew strong. The neighbouring Nitinat and the Uchucklesaht also banded with them to assist in pushing back their common enemies. The Ucluelet and others from across the Sound were almost decimated. Another decade went by. Although the Huu-ay-aht were successful and won many battles, they were frequently fighting, which played havoc with the seasonal round of food gathering. How can you focus on hunting a whale when you are preparing for battle? How can you let your guard down long enough to move with your family to the salmon stream when it is time to catch sockeye? The constant inability to relax made life tense for years. There was no peace anywhere. Finally a Ucluelet woman, a chief, appeared off the Huu-ay-ahts' shores. She came to ask that they stop the warring. Nanolinal listened and thought, "This is good, this chief is wise. She has spoken the very thoughts I have had myself."

The Huu-ay-aht agreed to stop the war, and to keep peace in the Sound. From that time on they would, at intervals, gather with the Ucluelet to eat together, to share salmon at the Sarita River, and to sing songs and tell stories. There would be no more war.

The peace survives to this day.

Chapter 5
Two Villages and their People Disappear

Today, we are well aware that the Pacific Northwest Coast is an area of the world in which seismic events occur on a regular basis. Earthquakes result from movement in the earth's crust. Pieces of this crust are known as plates. When two plates slide past each other, or one overtop another, they create shock waves that ripple through the rock, shaking the earth's surface. Two such plates lie off the shores of the Pacific Coast, and move regularly. The movement of the plates result in some 200 earthquakes recorded by scientists each year. Most of these quakes are small and often not noticed by the average person. But in the recent past, there have been several earthquakes of a magnitude sufficient to cause damage to a built environment, and to initiate movement of the ocean water. In 1963, a quake measuring 8.6 — on the Richter scale of 9 — occurred off the coast of Alaska. This quake triggered a huge tsunami, a wave that grew in intensity as it travelled across the ocean. When the tsunami reached Vancouver Island it surged up Alberni Inlet and spewed onto the land and the town of Port Alberni, causing massive destruction.

Archaeological excavations on the Pacific Coast show evidence of disruption in the occupation of First Nations resource sites and villages, and of profound geological upheaval. This information, combined with geophysical data gathered by scientists studying the earth's features, clearly indicates that in the centuries prior to contact with the outsider society, other significant earthquakes likely occurred, and lead back in time to a cataclysmic event that took place just over 300 years ago. Scientists agree that the evidence indicates a massive tsunami, some 10 to 15 metres in height, rolled across the Pacific Ocean and smashed into the shoreline along the outer coastal areas.

In Japan, on the opposite side of the Pacific Ocean, a tsunami also struck at this same time. Japanese survivors recorded the event as occurring in the year 1700. Based on the archaeological and geophysical evidence, the tsunami was triggered by a quake in the magnitude of a plus-nine. If the quake originated somewhere in the middle of the Pacific Ocean, it would have triggered waves radiating outwards, which would have rolled together, building in intensity until they hit solid land in both Japan and North America, and with devastating consequences. This, then, is the earthquake that triggered the huge wave recounted in the stories of First Nations, told over generations and recounted to others in the years since. The quake and tsunami changed life in the Huu-ay-aht world in a very dramatic way.

Once again, Chief Louie is the source for the following story. His account, unlike some of the other stories he told, is very brief. The reason for this is logical. He was passing on just the barest of information because that was all that existed. The tsunami was an event that only one person survived. Some additional details have been woven into this version to flesh out the rather terse recitation and to put the event in geographical context.

Annihilation

A great chief of the people living at Kee'hin had four sons, and he decided that it was time they marry. He sent his sons in a grand canoe procession, south along the coast to their neighbours who lived at the village of Clutus, located near the mouth of Pachena Bay. This was an important village, with a commanding view out to the Pacific Ocean and along the southern coast towards Pachena Point. The people of Clutus built their houses along both sides of an isthmus, a wise defensive position. They were great whalers, and had the best of both worlds: ready access to whales offshore, and an excellent vantage to spot drift whales. To the east lay the Pachena River, a good source for salmon in the autumn.

It was not a difficult journey for the sons; once the canoes rounded the rocky cliffs of Cape Beale, it was only a paddle of a few hours. The people at Clutus could see the canoes in the distance as they rounded the point and approached Keeha Bay. The canoes did not carry warriors painted for battle, for this was a social occasion.

As the canoes approached the village, small boys came out to greet them and helped pull the canoes onto the beach. The chief's house — the largest in the village — was clearly visible to the Kee'hin men, but as was the custom, they remained on the beach to begin the marriage ceremony. It was to last four days. There they sat on the beach and made overtures to the chief, whose name was Hayoqwis'is, which means "Ten-on-head-on-beach." Chief Hayoqwis'is received his name as a reflection of his whaling abilities, having beached 10 humpback whales at a single time.

As the highest ranking person, Hayoqwis'is had authority over this large village of Clutus and also over the smaller villages at Anacla, at the mouth of the river, and at Malsit, located just a little farther along the coast high atop a steep bank. Malsit was a good place to use as a base for halibut fishing. Chief Hayoqwis'is also claimed authority over the region south of Malsit, down to the territory controlled by the Nitinat people.

As the ceremony unfolded, the Kee'hin sons outlined to

Hayoqwis'is their reason for visiting. "We wish to purchase a bride," the eldest son explained. "Our father has sent us to you to find a wife from among your daughters. It will be good for us both to have ties of kinship between our groups."

Hayoqwis'is replied, "Yes, I agree it would be a wise thing to do, to unite our houses in marriage. But you must understand, my daughter is very precious to me. Her happiness is also important. I want to know that the man she will marry is worthy of her, not just because of his birthright, but because he is a strong man, and capable of leading his people. I consent to give my daughter in marriage to the man who proves himself worthy enough."

Thus the chief outlined a series of topati, or tests of strength and endurance, which would prove who among the four sons was worthy of his daughter. One of the topati was a broad jump. To earn Hayoqwis'is's daughter, one had to successfully jump four fathoms (approximately eight meters). This contest took place on a rocky shore at Clutus. The sons of the Kee'hin chief took their turns. The younger brother was the first to make the jump, but as he landed, his face smashed against the cliff and he broke his head and died. Eventually another brother succeeded, and by passing the topati, he earned the eldest daughter of the chief as his bride. The canoes left almost immediately for Kee'hin.

Sometime afterwards, at night, while the people in Clutus slept, the earth began to shake. The houses on the sandy beach swayed and the cedar boards shifted. By the time the people awoke — if they awoke at all — it was chaos. Beneath them, the sand sifted and turned to liquid; all their houses flattened and fell into the sand. There was no time to get into the canoes, and no way to make the distance from their houses to the water, for now all was liquid. Canoes floated out to the ocean while the villagers slid beneath the sand. And soon, very soon, the tide that pulled back from the beach and released the canoes brought in to the beach a wave almost as high as the cliffs on the southern mouth of the bay.

The wave, which must have glistened in the moonlight, crested and crashed as it hit the land, its power splintering the mighty fir and spruce trees in the forest well beyond the village site. As it sucked back with a tidal strength never before imagined, the wave took with it the forest, the animals, the rocks, and the entire village. All were killed, none remained living among those who had gone to sleep that night in the village of Clutus.

On the cliffs south of the bay, in the village of Malsit, the houses were built upon rock, not sand. As the earth shook, these houses swayed and some of the cedar planks and ridge-poles fell, but that was all. When the tsunami came, the people of Malsit were not swept out to sea, for their village was higher than the wave. But this was a small village, with not many people in it. Some of the people were out whaling, and these people, the ones out on the ocean, were also lost.

Other Huu-ay-aht villages were swept away or damaged. All along the coast people died. Those who survived woke to a world that would never be the same. Gone were many of their houses and canoes, much of their food, their grease, their smoked fish, and their dried berries. It was terrible devastation. With the loss of the people came also a loss of history, and in the continuity of traditions.

From Clutus, only the eldest daughter of the chief, the one who had left by canoe, survived. She was now married to the son of a Kee'hin chief. She never dreamed, as she was carried by canoe to her new home, that soon she alone would hold the rights and prerogatives of her father and his people. To the Kee'hin people she brought the territory extending from the Nitinat boundary up to Clutus. Thus the Kee'hin chief assumed control over a larger territory, and over the survivors at Malsit.

The devastation wrought that night in 1700 necessitated great change in the social structure of the Huu-ay-aht people. The losses of life, possessions, and food sources stripped local groups of much of their effectiveness. There were much fewer people, and many were without homes or food. The villages no longer had security of numbers, and in order to survive, new alliances had to be made. Previously independent people had to move from their now isolated circumstances to a closer proximity with others. This dramatic change in the social set-up was echoed throughout Barkley Sound

Cape Beale Underworld
An earthquake — possibly the same one that triggered the

tsunami that annihilated Clutus — wiped out the people living at Cape Beale. But the earthquake is just part of the story of Cape Beale's people. This story, which features a young whaling chief named Si'xpa'tskwin (meaning hunter-of-humpback-whales), comes from Chief Louie.

It all began one day, when Si'xpa'tskwin and three other young chiefs were out hunting. They followed a bear into its cave and then went far inside, beyond the opening. Deep within the cave it got lighter, and soon these four young chiefs found themselves in a wonderful land, a good country with a plentiful salmon river. They walked towards the river, and there killed many salmon, which they carried home in packs on their backs. These salmon were the type known as winter-springs.

Upon returning, the chiefs made sure that representatives from every house came to take a share of the salmon. In this way they distributed their wonderful bounty evenly among the villagers. Around the fire that night the young men told their remarkable story.

"A land beneath the earth? And one filled with salmon and forests?" asked the villagers. "Let's go and see for ourselves." So they nominated 10 young men to go to the cave the following day. These men, too, saw the good country, as well as birds — amazing birds called cheehayit'a. The 10 men walked around in this extraordinary land to get a better sense of it, and then speared some salmon and returned home.

The next day, everybody at Cape Beale wanted to go to

this marvellous place, and to see for themselves how easily the salmon could be caught. It seemed like a dream come true. For the people at Cape Beale, living as they did on a rocky headland, access to salmon rivers was limited. They had negotiated an arrangement with another group to use a spot on the Sarita River to gather salmon, but this was only seasonal. The fact that they might have access to their own private, albeit underground, salmon river was almost too good to be true.

Nearly every man lined up to see the cave. Those who were married went with their wives, many also took blankets and other items. Si'xpa'tskwin would not go this time, for something did not feel right, and he told his father so.

"Please father, do not go, it is not right to go. Listen to me please."

Neither Si'xpa'tskwin or his father went, but most of the others did go. They walked inside the cave for days, eventually coming out at the Sarita River after having passed through the bowels of the earth — for the river they had followed was under the earth. It was there, in this river, that the winter-spring salmon spawned. The people decided that they would prefer living in a land with abundant salmon. The Sarita was not theirs, but this underground river was their own discovery, so they stayed beneath the ground. Some 200 people never returned to Cape Beale. Only a handful of young adults, the children, and elders, along with Si'xpa'tskwin and his father, remained at the village.

After several days had passed, a few of the remaining villagers decided that they would join the others at the magical country. "Surely it must be a perfect place, otherwise they could have returned by now. We'll go tomorrow."

But before they had time to pack up, the land began to shake. It was an earthquake that caused widespread destruction. It flattened the hillside, and a landslide of mud and rock poured over the opening to the cave and tunnel. There was now no way the remaining villagers could follow their family members, and no way for the 200 people in the cave to return. These people became a ghost people, and could be seen now and then only as apparitions. They were trapped underground, and became wild.

Most of the young men had gone to the cave, and these were the whalers. Without their whaling chiefs and whaling crews, the villagers could not catch whales. They had to move, and to start afresh elsewhere. So they put what they owned into the big whaling canoes and paddled to the Sarita River. Next they moved up the river to a place called Ferns-On-Beach, and there they set up a new village. From this spot they could fish for dog salmon, enough for their winter food.

But then Si'xpa'tskwin saw another black bear. Again he was out with three other young men, and again they followed the bear for a while, thinking it might lead them into its lair, and that this would be profitable. They had their bows and arrows and were quite prepared. After a while, the bear headed up the Sarita, looked back, and saw that it was being followed. But still it continued its lumbering gait, seeming not to care. A little further on, though, the bear slowed, stooped down, and entered into a hole.

Well, Si'xpa'tskwin and the others paused for a second — hadn't this already happened before, and with quite devastating consequences? But curiosity got the better of them and they followed the animal. Into the hole they crawled. It was dark, but even so, there was a steady breeze coming from farther within. The young men ventured far beyond the opening, and soon the hole became a tunnel and they could stand inside. Curious, and emboldened by the breeze, the men continued down the dark passage, convinced that soon they would come up elsewhere on the riverbank. For surely the breeze they felt on their skins meant an opening to the outside.

Down, down they walked, and then, startling them ahead in the dark, they saw the shining eyes of the bear. Suddenly they became very tired and lay down on the dry earth to sleep. Upon awakening, refreshed and energized, they continued on, again seeing the shining eyes of the bear in the distance down the tunnel. Eventually the breeze got stronger. Then, much to their surprise, they came out not on the riverbank near their new village, but in that same underground wonderful land. It seemed the tunnel was connected to the one they had followed from Cape Beale.

Amazingly, it was daylight within the bowels of the earth, and the young men could see the abundant winter-springs, and the perfect land to live in. Excitedly they caught two salmon each and carried them on their backs, away from this place, back into the tunnel. They had to stop several times to sleep, for it was a longer distance back than they had realized on their journey in. It was dark and late by the time they reached home. Si'xpa'tskwin woke his father, and the others awoke their families. They stayed up all night, roasting the winter-spring salmon on sticks around the fire and talking about this new land. The idea, of course, was that if the underground land could be reached from this new cave, then the missing villagers could be found. Moreover, since the underground land was rich and plentiful, they could all go to live there. That way everyone would be reunited.

The next morning, every last villager resolved to go, including Si'xpa'tskwin, who this time convinced his father to go, too. Everyone gathered up their belongings. It took quite some time to pack and prepare. The only things not going to the underworld were the whaling canoes, which the villagers left on their sides on the beach. By nightfall, all had wiggled into the cave and set off underground. .

Later, neighbours of the villagers came upon the whaling canoes and wondered why they lay abandoned on the beach. To their amazement, not a soul was in the village. But footprints led up and along the river's edge. As these neighbours followed the footprints, another large earth tremor occurred. The land shifted, the trees swayed and cracked. It was frightening, but the neighbours persisted, and followed the footsteps to where they ended, rather abruptly, at a spot on the river that was much changed. The land had given way, and now a waterfall lay where none had before. This is the place called Took'ool. And it was here that the opening to the underworld was sealed forever.

Chapter 6
Whales and Whaling

"Whales wear clothes, like people, only the clothes they wear are skin and blubber and fins. They put these clothes on during the day, but at night, go back to their homes under the water and take these coats off. That is why whales are not often seen at night, and why the hunters have to be on the ocean by dawn when the whales first leave their houses and come to the ocean surface."

ith this explanation, an elder might initiate discussions with children about the Huu-ay-aht world, and about the place of animals within it. Whales were a significant part of human life because their bodies fed the tribes, their blubber and grease providing important nutrition.

Not all Huu-ay-aht people had the right to hunt whales. It was a sacred privilege, inherited by certain men within certain families. A great whaler was often also a chief, so his status was doubly large. Success in whaling came not just with luck, or with skill in harpooning, but through adequate spiritual preparation that focussed the mind for the danger of the hunt, and tuned it to the nuances of whale behaviour to get close to the whale without alarming it in any way. This ability was obtained through ritual purification and prayer, and by dedicating one's life to success in the hunt.

Whales are powerful and intelligent creatures. A whaler and his crew had to prepare themselves to be strong, both spiritually and physically, in order to be worthy of hunting the whale and to be successful at it. A whaler performed "oosimich," a purificatory bathing ritual. Oosimich was designed to toughen the physical body and to cleanse it of the human scent, as the warm, sweaty human body was disliked by the spirits. It was important not to anger the whale by being contaminated with unclean things that it could smell. So the whaler would go to his sacred spot and perform the bathing rituals. For four nights during the waxing of the moon, he bathed in cold fresh water and scrubbed his body with bundles of nettles and secret plants. During each session, he prayed that the whale would come close alongside his canoe. Then for four nights during the waning of the moon, he bathed at a secluded spot at sea. He swam counterclockwise, moving slowly like a whale — floating, diving, and blowing. Every four circuits he came out of the water to scrub his body with plants and to pray.

Whaling Canoes

Whalers had specific whaling canoes that were shaped to fit the function. It was important that they be made well, so they would glide evenly through the water. Like the whalers, the canoes had to be purified and remain clean. Whaling canoes were never drawn up on the beach or dragged down to the water, because if they were, they would come in contact with human smells, or touch rotting things on the sand. Instead, the canoes were carried down to the water on lifting poles.

Whaling canoes were made of red cedar and measured 10 metres or more in length, and could be two metres wide. Some of the best cedar was found near Kee'hin, but strong, tall, ancient cedar was plentiful throughout Huu-ay-aht territory. The process for making a canoe involved many steps, the first being selection of the best tree, ideally found near the edge of the forest, or near enough to be hauled out on rollers. Canoes were carved out of the tree trunk, not constructed of planks or boards. Once the tree was selected, it had to be felled. In the days before the outsiders provided metal, trees were felled using tools of stone, bone, and hardwood. Once a tree was on the ground, men removed the branches and bark. With the tree trunk clear, the canoe makers used wedges to help split the wood along the grain, and shaped the hull first. The inside was dug and carved out next.

Whaling canoes and a busy beach, Cha'pis, 1902

Great care was spent getting the correct thickness in the walls and floor of the canoe so that it would sit straight in the water and be balanced when paddled by its crew of eight — a harpooner, a steersman, and six paddlers.

Normally, the tree was felled in the autumn and the canoe was roughed out over the winter months and finished off in the spring. Then the canoe had to be moved from where it lay on the forest floor. This was a complex process involving logs propped beneath the canoe as it was pushed along on rollers to the beach, where the final phases would be completed.

The Hunt

The whaling season began each April with the northward migration of the mah'ak, or California gray whales. Si'xpa'ox, or humpback whales, mostly came in the summer, as did eehtop (the right whales) and kotsqu (the sperm whales). After performing oosimich, the whaler would call together his crew, and they would set forth before dusk so as to be out far from the shore before the dawn. Sometimes a whale was sighted, signalling that a pod might be travelling through, but often, too, the whaler would dispatch the canoe on the basis of a prophetic dream.

It could take a long time to get close to the whales, as they were usually quite a distance from land. Once on the hunting grounds, it often took equally long to situate the canoe so that it would be in the best position for harpooning a whale. Ideally the canoe would be on the left side of the whale as it breached on the surface of the ocean, and then the harpoon could be thrust just as the whale began to submerge with the flukes on the upswing. By positioning in this fashion, when the harpoon pierced the whale, the whale would react by swinging away from the canoe, not into it. This was a very dangerous operation. Whalers could not right an overturned canoe, and they were much too far away from land to survive the ocean temperatures. If successful in the kill, the whalers then needed to prevent the whale from sinking, and faced a marathon operation to manoeuvre the carcass to land, ideally to the village beach.

Whales and Whaling

Drift Whales

Like all animals, whales have a life cycle. When they die they do not sink right away. Instead, gasses quickly form inside them, making their carcasses buoyant. They float, buffeted by the wind and tide, often for some time before they either rot and sink, or wash up upon the shore. A whale that has washed up onshore is called a hon'i, or drift whale. It might be found any time during the year and does not appear just by chance, but because a chief had been diligent in his oosimich.

The right for drift whales belonged to the chief who owned the hahoothlee, the ocean or beach area where the carcass was found, or to the man who owned the rights to drift whales, which could be separate from ownership of territory. Once ownership was established, a strict protocol had to be followed. This protocol dictated the division of the carcass. The chief received the first piece, the saddle of the back near the fin. Then the harpooner and the other chiefs each took their pieces of blubber. The crew of the whaling canoe, or the individuals who helped tow in the drift whale, then received their pieces. The remaining skin and blubber was divided up amongst the villagers according to rank. Delicacies such as the tongue, lower jaw, flippers, and flukes were also distributed according to rank.

The two whaling stories included in this chapter come from a man whose name is recorded only as William. To date, relatively little is known about him, except that he was born around 1870 and had both Huu-ay-aht and Tseshaht ances-try. In 1913 and 1914, William was one of several cultural advisors consulted by anthropologist Edward Sapir. Based on the number of histories and narratives he provided to Sapir, it is clear that William was very knowledgeable concerning many details of traditional life in Barkley Sound. His father, whose name was Haq'to'a, was half Huu-ay-aht, and it is from him that William learned Huu-ay-aht narratives.

A Whale, and a Story

Chief Si'xpa'tskwin of Cape Beale was always trying to better himself as a whaler. He performed oosimich, he fasted, and he prayed. One day, he determined that if he had better eye-sight, and could see far into the distance, he could lead his people to more whales. But how could he accomplish this? As he pondered the situation, he looked at all the other animals in his world. Many of them had very keen eyesight and because of this could protect themselves well. Others had great skill in locating food. He was most impressed by birds. He knew that the eagles and hawks were amazing hunters. From high in the sky they spotted their prey, and then from these great distances swept down with deadly accuracy. Si'xpa'tskwin resolved that he would do what he could to improve his eyesight by borrowing the eyes of a bird. He took the eyes of an osprey and worked with them for many hours. Finally he was successful in finding a way to alter and then combine them with his own eyes.

Now when Si'xpa'tskwin looked out over the water he could see far in the distance. He was most happy with his new eyes and spent the rest of the day looking out to sea, searching the horizon. He searched, of course, for whales. Looking south one day, Si'xpa'tskwin saw a drift whale way, way out. Without his new eyes he would never have had this power.

Several young men were sitting on the rocks on the beach with Si'xpa'tskwin. He said to them, "Look, there on the horizon, there are many birds, seagulls, eating the whale."

The other men looked but did not see it. "Are you sure?" they questioned. "We can't see anything, and we don't really believe that you have the eyes of an osprey."

"Yes, the whale is there, and we should set our canoes in the water and tow the whale in to the village."

"But I don't know if it is worth it for the bother," one man said. "It is only your word that you can see this whale."

"Let's go and see it," another replied. And so they did. They lifted a big canoe down the beach and 10 of the young men got into it. They began paddling. With so many paddlers, the canoe sprinted forward through the waves. On they paddled. Every now and then Si'xpa'tskwin would stand up and look ahead on the horizon, checking that they were on course. The young men paddled in the direction he told them, for they still could see nothing in the water.

"It's close now, it isn't far now," Si'xpa'tskwin said as they paddled, going farther and father out to sea. Soon Cape Beale went down over the horizon. Now it was late afternoon, then

93

it became evening. Finally, the young men could see something in the distance.

"Sure enough, there are many birds."

Then they saw it, floating on the sea. It was indeed a dead whale. They manoeuvred the canoe close to the carcass. They were extremely tired and stopped paddling.

"You climb up onto it and cut off a chunk of blubber," they said to Si'xpa'tskwin. He climbed onto the whale and cut off a chunk. The young men looked at each other, and then looked around. It was then that they realized the situation they were in. It was a long, long way to the shore. They could not even see the land, they were so far off it. Yes, Si'xpa'tskwin had amazing eyesight to have seen this drift whale, but what had he done bringing them out so far from home? How would they ever have the strength to drag the carcass to shore? Why had they kept paddling without thinking of the fix he was getting them into?

"There is no way that we can bring this whale home with us," one young man whispered to another. "We are far, too far out to sea and will die in the trying. I for one think we should just leave Si'xpa'tskwin here with this whale he so foolishly led us to. Let him bring it in on his own, or die trying."

The canoe drifted, and the young men became angry that they had been led into such danger. "Let's go home now. Let him stay right on the whale."

They paddled off, these nine young men, and abandoned Si'xpa'tskwin on the carcass. They arrived ashore at the village at Cape Beale late at night when everyone was asleep, but by then they had their story all figured out so that the next day they could explain what had happened.

"Oh, somebody took him," they said. "A canoe came alongside of us, perhaps they were hunting whale. They were people of another tribe, but we don't know which tribe. They took him from our canoe into theirs. There were many in their canoe and they had many weapons. It was impossible to fight them. So the only thing to do was to flee. It must be that these people had heard of Si'xpa'tskwin's eyes and wanted his sight for themselves."

The people mourned their chief, who had been so mysteriously taken. But Si'xpa'tskwin was not dead. The wind began to blow, first from the east, and then from the west. The whale carcass with its stranded passenger drifted even farther out to sea. Si'xpa'tskwin prayed for his life, he prayed that he would go home. He was on the ocean for 10 days, and during this time he heard voices that spoke to him.

"Do not cry, you are slowing us down."

"If you are cold, dig in to the blubber and fit yourself down into the hole. Cover your head with the skin, and you will be dry from the rains."

"If your mouth is parched, suck on some blubber. If you are hungry, eat some of the blubber."

In this manner, Si'xpa'tskwin survived. He received good advice from the voices and did not die. All the while he prayed that he be set on land once more. Si'xpa'tskwin knew that spirits were assisting him, but they did not show themselves in true form. At times he thought he saw another canoe with paddlers towing the whale, and once he saw an orca pushing the carcass along. He had many visions and listened to all he was told. Eventually a voice whispered that the whale was now beached on the rocks beside his village. The voice then told him where to find a ball that he should throw at those who had left him for dead. When the time came, Si'xpa'tskwin threw the ball, which twirled and spun in the air. It landed on the rocks near the carcass and kept spinning. At once it began making a wolf-whistling sound, and at this moment all nine of the young men who had abandoned Si'xpa'tskwin doubled up in pain and died. In this way the spirits helped the chief take revenge on those who had betrayed him.

Crystals and Strength

Each Huu-ay-aht whaler has his own sacred spots for oosimich, but one of the most sacred spots of all is the mountain known as o'quatsqa, which translates as "Bladder-head." Named for the profile it presents from certain angles, this mountain resembles the inflated seal skins that are used as floats when whaling. The whole of this mountain is sacred, from the valleys surrounding it, to the slopes leading up to its peak and the cliffs that run down to the ocean. The red cedar that grows on this mountain has special qualities not found in cedar from other territories. The mountain is also special because it has many hidden spots that are perfect for performing oosimich. For this reason, it is a destination point. But Bladder-head has another level of importance. It is here, on and around this mountain, that an unusual group of supernatural spirits reside. Their power can be dangerous, so travel on the mountain is not for the uninitiated.

The caves of Bladder-head house something quite marvellous and rare. These are he'na', supernatural quartz crystals that grow to a huge size. Very responsive to movement, the he'na' often sway back and forth, and at times vibrate, emitting an unusual humming sound. The louder the humming, the greater the power. The ball that Si'xpa'tskwin threw at his betrayers hummed and emitted a whistling sound because it was a crystal, given to him by the spirits who helped him bring the drift whale to shore.

The valleys approaching the mountain are where the y'ai' can sometimes reveal themselves. But it is only an observant and quickly responsive person who will see them. Farther up the mountain slopes, the y'ai' hide. These y'ai' are supernatural spirits who resemble men but have tufts of feathers projecting up from either side of their heads. They are usually seen in groups, in the magical number combinations of 4 or 10, and they emit a shrill sound like children make at play. It is important to be strong spiritually, for the y'ai' have been known to kill without mercy those who encounter them without proper preparation. Y'ai' dispense power, and can infuse one who is ready with special skills in whaling or doctoring, in the arts, and in song or with wealth.

It seems as though the y'ai' are seen more often than these next two creatures. The Michtach are odd-shaped mallard-like birds with beautiful feathers and supernatural powers that people can obtain by snatching part of their plumage. They are among the most unusual supernatural creatures, and accounts of seeing a Michtach, let alone successfully catching a feather, are exceedingly rare. They fly with lightning speed and can swoop down unexpectedly, but it is their noise that is most reported. There are so many of them hidden away that when they flap their wings it makes a thunderous sound which can be overwhelming and deafening. A whaler might visit the mountain many times in his life and hear the Michtach, but never get close enough to see them.

A supernatural creature also resides on the bluffs of Bladder-head Mountain. This is the ch'och'oht'a, which translates as "stretched down from a bluff onto the rocks." According to the elders, this creature "is said to look like a big Octopus, and can give good power for whale-hunting. It is extremely difficult to get. When you get near, he goes right up the bluff out of reach so you cannot get a piece of him for a charm ... he always stays on rocks. He is black, like a whale, and has many eyes like an octopus."

The following story, told by William to Edward Sapir in 1914, is an important narrative because it is one of only a few sources of traditional information about the sacred mountain that lies within Huu-ay-aht territory. The story shows us just how important the mountain, with its supernatural power and spirit creatures, is in the quest for whaling prowess.

An Unlikely Whaler
The village of Yashitko'a lies far inland from the mouth of Barkley Sound, near Coleman Creek. The people of this village were expert canoe makers. They were a very rich people because the work they did was in demand from others and they could trade canoes for almost everything they needed. But in this village was a young chief who did not like it that their neighbours made fun of them. Whaling was a prestigious pursuit, while making canoes from red cedar trees, although requiring great skill, was not. The Yashitko'a traded for sea mammals and therefore had no need to oosimich. This made them humble when among those who did. When the Yashitko'a people visited their neighbours, they took gifts of cedar boards for making houses. These boards, made of the finest and straightest grain cedar, were very well formed but rather pedestrian.

"Don't bother to look in their canoes," the neighbours would say when they came visiting. "They have only brought us boards for gifts."

The young Yashitko'a chief said to his father, "I want to become a whaler. I want to catch many whales so our village can be proud whalers, not just proud canoe makers."

"Well," his father answered, "to learn to be a whaler, you must make preparation. You must pray and prepare your body and mind. You must bathe in the sacred places, you must fast and stay vigilant, training your mind. This will be a commitment, my son. Are you ready for such a step?"

The young man was ready, and he started oosimich, bathing and rubbing his body with special plants so that he would become strong. He did this every day for a year. At the end of the year he sat beside the small fire that he had built to warm himself. He covered his shoulders with a bearskin robe and stared into the fire. All at once he saw a creature creep to the fire and steal the flames away. The young chief followed this creature and tried to catch it, to reclaim the fire. But it seemed that whatever he did, he could not quite catch up to whatever it was that ran ahead of him. As much as he tried, the creature was too quick, and he could only follow at some distance behind it. The creature led him to the mountain called Bladder-head. When he got there, the young man became dizzy and slumped down on the forest floor, passed out. But something brought him back to consciousness and made him wake up.

As he opened his eyes he saw a strange creature, not the creature that had stolen his fire, but another. This one was black and had many hands. In a flash it jumped up the bluff and was gone.

"This is too strange," thought the young man.

"Whatever it is has left me here and I am unable to follow." He returned home.

Again, he began oosimich, and again he bathed and prayed, strengthening his body and mind. He had visions. In the visions he saw another creature, this one looked a bit like a cormorant, but made a noise like an otter, and also like a mallard duck. The young man told his father about these visions.

"Well my son, you must now continue oosimich for another four days. After this you must walk and travel to the mountain called Bladder-head. You must seek out this creature you have seen, for it is a Michtach. This is a very special being, and one that can provide you with powers also. Each one has powers for different purposes. You must find the Michtach for whalers."

Again the young man walked and reached the valley beside the mountain. He saw all sorts of strange birds flying about. "Surely they are supernatural," he thought to himself. "They sound and look so unusual." He watched carefully, hoping to be able to get close to one of them. But they were very aware of him and did not reveal themselves fully. It was very frustrating for the young chief, and in the end his patience ran out. He became disheartened and returned home, where some of the villagers chided him because he kept coming back with no power. It was embarrassing to listen to their laughter and teasing, but he remained committed and resolved to try again.

Once more the young man performed oosimich, and once more he spoke with his father, who encouraged him in this pursuit. This time, the young man asked that his mother pack four strips of dried blubber that he could take with him for nourishment. He then went upstream along the river and walked all day until dark. He stopped several times to bathe, and to tear four small strips off the blubber, which he ate. It took a long while to get to the mountain. He wanted to make sure his body was pure and that his mind was protected from harm. By eating and sucking on the blubber, he was protected by the spirit of the whale and so he felt strong. Then, as he approached the bluffs, he encountered the ch'och'oht'a, and again it sped away from him up the mountain. Discouraged, the young man returned home yet another time.

Once more he prepared. But this time he asked his mother for advice. She looked at her son and saw how strong he was. His body was toughened, his eyes bright, and his heart good.

"Maybe," she began, "maybe it is your breath that the beings smell. It gives you away. These beings can smell you and have warning that you are near to them. You offend them with your smell and they know that you are not worthy. You must disguise the smell of your breath. To do this, my son, you must fast for ten days. Drink only water and then set out once more."

Ten days of fasting focussed the young man. He was now very determined, and his mind was made up. This was his fourth trip, and he would not return until he had accomplished the task. This time, he strode out purposefully. When he reached the base of the bluff he stopped and stood very quietly. After a long while he saw movement off to the side, and still he waited. The ch'och'oht'a crept along the rocks and did not appear to notice him. Slowly, ever so slowly, he crouched down, preparing to spring towards the creature. Still the creature made no indication that it had seen him.

"I must be worthy," he reminded himself. "I must not offend the ch'och'oht'a with my smell, or my breath."

He judged the timing, and in one quick movement grabbed for the creature. This time he caught the tip of one of its arms. He held tight as the creature wiggled and squirmed. With mighty strength, the creature pulled away, but left behind in the young man's hands some pieces of its tentacle.

"Success!" he cried aloud. "Thank you Great Spirit for preparing me to be worthy." And with that thought, the young man carefully wrapped his power in a soft skin and turned back for the homeward journey. Just outside the village, close to his house, the young man found a secret spot in which to hide his power, for it was forbidden to take the charm into a house. He then entered the house and all his family gathered around him. They could tell from his demeanour that he was changed, and now had supernatural power.

Four days passed. On the fourth day, the young man advised, "Today the humpbacks will come into the bay."

The young man went with others from the village down to the beach and into the canoes. That day, he caught four whales, killing each one with only a single spear thrust. The young man was now a proven whaler. He had achieved his aspiration, and now his village could be proud. Not only were the Yashitko'a people famous as canoe makers, but their young chief also had great powers as a whaler. They would never be hungry because he could charm the whales right into the bay.

Chapter 7
The World Changes Forever

In 1874, George Blenkinsop, hired by the government of Canada, travelled to Barkley Sound on the west coast of Vancouver Island. His job was "to gather information on Native needs and desires with regard to land" as a preparation for the allocation of "Indian Reservations," which would be undertaken by a duly appointed Indian Reserve Commission. Blenkinsop spent three months travelling by boat and on foot. During this time, he interviewed the chiefs of each tribe to learn about their use of the land for food gathering, their traditions in hunting both on the ocean and in the forest, and all manner of resource extraction. He recorded the names of each family in each lodge, as well as the age and sex of all family members. This was the first formal census of Barkley Sound, for these First Nations had no such need to record their family information on paper. They had traditional historians who kept track.

But the government needed the paper records. The purpose, of course, was to see how many people lived in the area, and on what land they resided. With this information in hand, government officials could then send the reserve commissioner and surveyors to measure out the land reservations for the First Nations. This land would be held in trust for them, while other adjacent lands could be purchased or pre-empted by the outsiders: the white immigrants, the merchants, the entrepreneurs, and the timber barons.

Blenkinsop was a patient and experienced man. He wanted to make sure he understood how Huu-ay-aht society worked and how the land and its resources were used. He asked many questions and spoke to chiefs from different villages. He could see that the large territory in which the Huu-ay-aht lived was not all filled with people. In fact, he wrote to Ottawa to say that based upon his observations of the size and quantity of abandoned villages, "incontestably the population of Barkley Sound must have been at no very remote period, ten times its present number." He also noted that people lived in villages on a seasonal basis, following the food cycle and the weather. Thus, he wrote, "It is difficult to obtain an accurate accounting of the population because many of the people are between villages, or have just moved from one site to the next, and I have missed them." When Blenkinsop recorded his census, many of the large villages on the salmon-bearing rivers were not inhabited, because, of course, it was summer and most salmon had not yet returned to the rivers to spawn.

The census results proved what First Nations had known for some time: their once robust population was but a shadow of its former self. Yes, natural cataclysms such as earthquakes, flooding, and violent storms had taken lives. And yes, the human dynamic and the friction of the many tribes within Barkley Sound were taken into account, as groups jostled for position, for rights to hunting areas, salmon streams, and drift whales. But what Blenkinsop was speaking about was not a minor or general weakening of the population base. He was seeing the remnants of what had been populous tribes, tribes whose decreased numbers echoed the experiences of other Nuu-chah-nulth peoples in Clayoquot and Nootka Sounds, and indeed along the Pacific Coast generally.

Today, experts and historians estimate that by the mid 19th century, the population of First Nations on the coast of British Columbia had been decimated by at least 90 percent. This massive depopulation occurred within a single life-span and was a direct result of contact with the outsider society — the explorers and the early maritime fur traders — who brought infectious diseases such as measles, whooping cough, tuberculosis, influenza, syphilis, and the most deadly of all, smallpox. First Nations had no immunity to these diseases, which were unknown in their world.

In the few years after Cook's 1778 sojourn at Nootka Sound, to Simon Fraser's overland journey to the coast in 1808, it was obvious that the area's First Peoples had been stricken by epidemics that had travelled the length of the coast. The sicknesses had passed from the outsiders to First Nations, but then spread through trade and contact between the First Nations themselves. The first European reference to introduced disease dates from 1791, when the log from the ship *Columbia* records that smallpox was present among the Nuu-chah-nulth: "Twas evident that these Natives had been visited by that scourge of mankind. The Smallpox ...The face of the Chief bears evident marks."

In 1788, John Meares, a fur trader, calculated the number of people under the authority of the major Nuu-chah-nulth chiefs in Barkley, Clayoquot, and Nootka Sounds. The total number came to 31,000. Even roughly dividing by three, this estimates a robust population within Barkley Sound itself. But in 1874, less than 100 years later, Blenkinsop was only able to confirm that 949 people lived in all of Barkley Sound. And of these, the once mighty Huu-ay-aht now numbered only 262.

An Huu-ay-aht account records a specific instance in which smallpox came to their territory. It was right at the end of the Long War, and the tribes in Barkley Sound had agreed to stop fighting. But, obviously, suspicions and uncertainty coloured people's perceptions regarding the motives of others.

Smallpox

The story begins when a ship came to N'aqowis, across from Bamfield Inlet. The ship did not anchor, but seemed instead to drift about as though no one was onboard. This was quite curious and out of character for these mamatni, or outsiders, who were usually so regulated and assertive. However, from the Huu-ay-aht perspective, custom demanded that they greet each visitor to their territory. As usual, they organized a procession of canoes that went out to the ship.

"Welcome!" they called as their canoes came close to the hull. But there was no answering call. Unworried, the villagers climbed aboard. When they stood on the deck and looked down the hatch, they saw that there was something very wrong with many of the white men, the sailors, for they were all groaning. The ship had come up the coast from San Francisco, and the captain told them that it had already stopped in at Yuquot and at Ahousat.

The captain turned to the Huu-ay-aht and said, "For seven days you will be well. Then you will get that sickness." The Huu-ay-aht did not know what the sickness was, as they had not seen it before. Within the seven days, they knew all about it, for this was smallpox. Many died. Out of 2000 adults, only 80 families survived.

The Huu-ay-aht grew suspicious. Why, if the crew had

been so sick, had the ship ventured into villages on the coast? Had they been seeking assistance, or had something more nefarious been planned? Some of the Huu-ay-aht thought it had been a deliberate exposure, and believed their enemies, the Clallam people, had directed the American sailors to come north.

Many Huu-ay-aht died over the next six months. Chief Louie's grandfather, who had not been on the ship, quickly moved his family to a mountain near Sarita Lake. By doing so, they escaped the smallpox. Eventually the sickness ended. There was much talk among the survivors, for all were convinced that the American captain had been hired to spread the disease. The Huu-ay-aht talked with the Ucluelet, who, until the close of the Long War, had been their bitter enemies. The Ucluelet, too, had suffered and were angry. Together, the two groups formed a war party and went to Clallam Bay to take revenge. Just how they did this, however, is unclear. It is not recorded whether the attack was successful, but with such a reduction in population, none of the survivors had the resources or abilities to mount and carry out an effective raid.

Outsiders Do Not Understand
In 1868, missionary Harry Guillod reported on an outbreak of smallpox among the Huu-ay-aht: "40 Huu-ay-ahts had died of the disease which was fast spreading ... those who were affected by it were so terrified that they were neglecting to lay in their winter's store of salmon, so that starvation would

probably ensue upon the disease." In 1882, Guillod was Indian Agent, and conducted his first actual census. He travelled throughout Barkley, Clayoquot, and Nootka Sounds and counted 3610 people, confirming a 90 percent reduction.

It is difficult to imagine the personal psychological impact, let alone the cultural impact, of losing 9 out of every 10 people within a 50-year period. Who would raise the children? Who would bury the dead? Who would own the rights and prerogatives if a family was wiped out? How would the oral history of the people survive? How would the intricate sharing of resources and communal gathering of foods continue? Who would teach the young men how to prepare themselves for catching whales? Who would build the canoes and dry the salmon?

Many proud and numerous lineages were swept away. The traditional independence of the local groups could not continue without enough people. Instead, the survivors forged alliances with neighbouring villages, sharing village sites and territories. The world of the Huu-ay-aht was forever changed.

The remaining peoples still held the rights to the traditional territories and privileges. They were hard pressed to make Blenkinsop understand that their system of land use and occupation required the large geographical areas of the territories they claimed. In Blenkinsop's view, the future for First Nations lay not in maintaining their old way of life, but in embracing the new order controlled by the outsider society and its government. The Huu-ay-aht and other nations were expected to develop agriculture, to grow potatoes, to plant fruit trees, and to tend the land at a specific spot. Blenkinsop and others of the day believed that the old ways would die out and that assimilation with the outsider society was not only desired, but inevitable.

Blenkinsop drew a map of Barkley Sound and placed on it the areas in which he found people situated. He did listen to the information they provided about the places that salmon and other foods were harvested, and took this into consideration. He recommended that the government surveyors measure out modest plots of land on whatever arable areas people happened to already live on, and also allow for small encampment areas on salmon rivers, and burials — lots of burials. The sizes of these recommended reserves were small, and often included infertile or inhospitable areas.

Peter O'Reilly was the Indian Reserve Commissioner who was sent to meet with representatives of the Huu-ay-aht. He steamed up from Victoria on a naval ship and arrived in Dodgers Cove on Diana Island on May 26, 1882. The next day, he recorded the following in his diary: "Had an interview with the chiefs of the Huu-ay-aht tribe. Afterwards accompanied by them I laid off a number of reserves nearly all for fishing purposes. Intended to go to Bamfield Cr. but could not, returned to Dodgers Cove." The following day was Sunday, and he remained onboard the ship writing letters home and observing the "day of rest." On Monday: "Up anchor at

5:45 am. A lovely morning. Laid out a reserve at Helby Island and then steamed to Bamfield Creek ... Worked hard all the day and anchored in Green Cove at 7:30 p.m." He was now out of Huu-ay-aht territory, and on to the next tribe's reservations. He spent a total of two days actually speaking with and visiting the Huu-ay-aht and their villages. On the basis of this intense experience he laid out 13 reserves (see map on page 12), which remain today the current lands allocated to the Huu-ay-aht.

The people were now forced onto 13 small plots of land, spread throughout their territory, and denied access to or use of most of their traditional sites. It is estimated that the Huu-ay-aht Indian Reserves today represent less than one percent of the territory they once controlled. These reserves were never given to the Huu-ay-aht, but held in trust for them by the government of Canada. Such a paternalistic view was intolerable for the Huu-ay-aht, but what could a formerly strong people do?

On May 8, 1914, Chief Louie and other Huu-ay-aht elders spoke to the members of the Joint Federal-Provincial Indian Commission when it came to Bamfield to meet with the Huu-ay-aht about their reserves. This was part of a larger trip in which the commissioners travelled around British Columbia to speak with all First Nations about the reservations that had been established between 1874 and 1912.

In the few scant hours they were there, the commissioners asked Chief Louie and other Huu-ay-aht chiefs questions about their land allotments. In the outsider community, there was some speculation that these reserves were too large for the needs of First Nations and should be cut back. Chief Louie was not impressed with the interchange. The commissioners posed very specific questions concerning the use of the land, asking for evidence of use that was not traditional to the Huu-ay-aht, but rather about agricultural use. They asked about seasonal villages, about gas boats, about sealing (which by then was outlawed), and about schooling. They did not seem to require in-depth responses, and in fact did not encourage detail. Finally, near the end of the interviews, Chief Louie made a point to illustrate the differences between Huu-ay-aht traditional fishing and the fishing practised by the Japanese and white people who had moved in and pre-empted or purchased land that was on the more significant of Huu-ay-aht sites. These people freely moved — without permission of the Huu-ay-aht, but with the protection of the outsider society — in the waters which had for generations been the prerogatives of chiefs.

"The cannery men are using a seine for their fishing," Chief Louie explained, "and they catch all the fish going up the Sarita River. They purchase a licence for the seine and they place the nets in such a manner that we in our gas boats trolling or, on our land at Numukamis, are unable to fish, for all the salmon are caught in the nets before they can swim up the river. This is a serious situation, for our people cannot catch the salmon we need because the seine nets catch the salmon. I worry for my people, and I worry for the survival of the salmon. Never before have such quantities of salmon been caught before they spawn. Tell me, will you do something about this?"

One commissioner replied, "This question of closing the mouths of streams by seines was discussed by the commission with the federal and provincial government fishery officers a short time ago."

The other commissioner then added: "We will take everything you have told us today into consideration, and will do what we can for you."

With that final remark, the representatives closed their books and adjourned the meeting. Chief Louie never received an answer. Fifty years later, his anger at that day remained unabated. Sitting in front of a microphone and a tape recorder, he paused in his storytelling to remind his listeners of these historical injustices. He spoke of his father's attempts to stop the surveyors, and of the hollow promises given by the commissioner and government officials.

"Now the government surveyors are taking our lands. They are putting us on tiny reservations, all these lands we owned. The lands surrounding us are literally taken away from us. Dr. Powell was head of the Indian Commission in 1874–76. My father went to the surveyor in 1875–76. He confronted him asking, 'How can you give us small piece of land in our own territory? What are you surveyors doing by taking and stealing our lands?'

"My father was very concerned but did not want to fight the government. He only asked how can they take our lands. The government said we wouldn't lose our lands and we would still have all the rights. You'll never be in need of wood. You'll still be able to use all your resources, such as cedar for making canoes. When you have to go into the forest you can still make your canoes. Whatever it takes to build. You can fall all the cedar you want for canoes or firewood, because this is your territory. If you want to build your long houses, shingles. The cedar is there for you to harvest. This is what Dr. Powell said in Victoria. The government will give you cattle, sheep, pigs — even give us chickens and let them multiply and make money on this livestock. Dr. Powell said this is good offering for us. [He] said we could have an easier way of living. Yet this never arrived, promise broken again, nothing came from Victoria. This is what the government now claims, that they have claimed our territories without even signing any papers or agreement. No documents. They were just telling us lies so they could benefit for themselves. All the chiefs witnessed this, fooling us in what they promised.

"The surveyors still went ahead and placed us on small reserves and stole our lands. All the money came from Ottawa, thousands and thousands of dollars, but we did not get any of it. We did not sell our lands. Because our lands are too valuable to our people. Yet the government never treated us right. They took our lands. Our chiefs never signed them away."

Chapter 8
Fur Sealing

he adult male northern fur seal weighs 270 kilograms and measures 2.5 metres long. In contrast, the female is tiny, weighing 45 kilograms. These remarkable animals live most of their lives in the ocean, coming onto land only to mate and give birth. Seals are resident from California to Alaska, and each spring a large population swims north, migrating to rookeries in the Pribilof Islands, where they breed. However, not all fur seals migrate to breed, some stayed all year in Huu-ay-aht territory. This was once an important benefit for the Huu-ay-aht, as it was much easier to hunt close to home.

Fur seals have a rich warm pelt. Given the damp, cold winters on the coast, these pelts were ideal for clothing. The large male animals also provided food for the people. In the Huu-ay-aht world view, it is crucial to keep the balance in nature, to ensure that human needs do not jeopardize or overpower those of nature. All is one. It is important to honour the life of the animal you kill for food. The way you respect the animal is to ensure there is no waste, that all of the animal is utilized once it is killed, and that it did not give its life needlessly.

Not every Huu-ay-aht man had the right to hunt seals. The right was given and handed down within families, as was the right to fish for salmon on particular spots on the river, as was the right to hunt whales. Those who held the rights also held the responsibility to be providers for others, and to share.

The Huu-ay-aht hunted seals using spears that measured four or five meters long and about three centimetres in diameter. The spears had a handle and two fastened-on prongs, one almost a metre long and the other half this length. The shafts were made of crab-apple wood, and the spear points were made of mussel shells, deer and elk horn parts, or stone. As trade goods came into the territory from the outsiders, metal commonly replaced these natural materials as the preferred spearhead.

Because the seals lived in the ocean, they were generally speared from canoes. These dugout cedar canoes were specially designed with flat bottoms for stability, flared gunwales on the bow to prevent water from splashing, and high vertical sterns. After contact, the Huu-ay-aht experimented by adding sails of canvas or cotton. This allowed the paddlers to rest when the wind was strong, and enabled the canoes to travel further offshore. The seals resident in Huu-ay-aht territory were also sometimes speared from shore as they basked on the rocks at low tide.

The first mamatni, or outsiders, saw a commercial use for the pelts of the fur seals, the sea otter, and furred land mammals. In many world centres, especially those in China and Europe, these furs became valued commodities. Thus a brisk maritime trade commenced between merchants who arrived on ships, and the coastal First Nations who exchanged fur pelts for beads, metal, cloth, and foodstuffs. As more ships arrived on the coast, the pressure to provide fur pelts for trade created a dilemma for the Huu-ay-aht and others. How could they maintain their world view when an extraordinary demand for furs from these outsiders pressured the community into compromising the balance of resource consumption?

No longer was their economy self sufficient, trading within First Nations and living off the bounty of nature. Now, new goods and food entered the picture, and outside influences (like the infectious diseases that killed so many) initiated change, but change that came so rapidly the Huu-ay-aht were swept up in it before they realized it could not be controlled.

As the quest for furs became big business, consortiums

based in San Francisco and Victoria financed a fleet of sailing vessels that followed the seals north, and killed them when they were most vulnerable — on land at the rookeries where they bred and gave birth. Huu-ay-aht people were in demand as sealers. The sailing vessels took their canoes and crew onboard with them as they sailed north. The sealers were paid for each seal speared, but not paid in cash, just in food-stuffs and trading goods. For several intense decades in the late 19th century, sealing provided a living for many Huu-ay-aht men. Young men grew up learning not the old ways, but the new ways of sealing — of hunting for goods instead of hunting for food. Not surprisingly, despite international attempts to regulate the carnage and killing at the rookeries, the once plentiful fur seals were soon in danger of extinction.

International interests, interests beyond the Huu-ay-aht world, interests of business, of investors, and of governments, came into play. By 1911, the big business of fur sealing was put under strict regulation controlled by American and Russian interests. Quotas and international law prevailed. The early settlers had valued the hunting skills of the Huu-ay-aht, as it was tricky business spearing seals from canoes and the Huu-ay-aht had perfected this work through generations of training. But these skills were no longer needed when guns became the preferred killing tool.

What had once been a pelagic, or ocean-based, hunt became strictly land based and regulated. Native sealers were left out, forbidden to go north on the boats. The people who had become dependent upon this outside employment now had no work. They had no means to purchase goods, and had grown away from the traditional ways of living self-sufficiently within their territory. A time of great hardship followed.

Written histories of sealing generally revolve around the non-aboriginal participants and focus on the businesses, the sealing captains, the consortiums, the international players, and the big money investments. Chief Louie, however, gives an account from the Huu-ay-aht perspective, and discusses his own personal odyssey.

"I was born in 1881 on the 15th of March at Dodger's Cove Island, that's where I was born. In 1894 I had my first experience in going out to the ocean in a sealing canoe to learn how to hunt for fur seals in our territory.

"When we hunted the fur seals we saved the pelts and meat, which was smoked and eaten fresh. This was our tradition to go for these fur seals, this all belongs to us, the people along the coast. We also used [the seals'] hides for our clothing. We did not have to go too far out in the sea because it was so plentiful. The fur seal and hair seal were sometimes some distance out in the ocean, but these seals had mated and bred right here in Huu-ay-aht territory. They didn't migrate north to have their young, although many others did — all along the coast right up to the Bering Sea. We had many seals that stayed in our territory and bred in our waters.

"When I started hunting fur seals I accompanied my

father and my older brother. I witnessed the way they speared these seals and soon, the way they hunted these seals. We only took what we needed, that is our way.

"But now two men came, traders, they came in schooners from Victoria. These traders came into our territory and offered the people rice and sugar and molasses in exchange for seals. Their prices for the seals were almost insulting. They used small teacups to measure. A small seal went for two cups of rice. One big fur seal went for three cups of molasses. A white whiskered seal, two cups of molasses or whatever you wanted to purchase in equal value of rice or sugar. These traders came for all the furs — for fur seals, beavers, and sea otter. Beaver went for half a cup of rice. Then they brought pants, cotton pants made in China, and the price rose — one seal for one pair of pants.

"Fur seal became big business. We hunted in our own territories. For me and my father, it was the Dodger's Cove area. Now the people hunted seals for trade, we became dependent upon the traders, and the pay for each seal was so small, we killed more than we ever had before. Soon people along the coast had lots of rice, sugar, molasses, and pants. But the seals were scarce.

"The white traders were the ones to benefit by all the fur seals. They got wealthy. As long as the seal market was on, we never got a fair shake, because the traders then sold the seals for high prices in Victoria. White people wanted the fur — and the oil — and paid the traders with money. The traders never paid us money, just rice and sugar and such.

"A few years later, though, Captain Victor Jacobson arrived. The name of his schooner was *Kwachisht*. He asked the people to come with him to hunt in the great ocean. Four of our canoes with a kuu-us crew went in the schooner with him. We went to the Bering Sea to spear seals. Captain Jacobson paid us with money for the seals we speared. The price from Captain Jacobson was $2.50 for a fur seal up to 4 or 5 feet in length. He understood our heritage. He told us that he wanted to buy these seals with money and to be honest with us.

"He stationed his schooner off Dodger's Cove. My father and Captain Jacobson became close, my father started looking after the sales of these seals. Soon I started as a crewmember on the schooner and I went with Captain Jacobson every year to hunt seals in the Bering Sea. We brought our canoes on the deck of the schooner when we sailed north, and then when we reached the breeding grounds we lowered the canoes into the water. Two men in each canoe. Lots of our people went with the schooners from Victoria. They did this for a living. It was very common work because of our talent for canoeing and hunting. So when I was growing up I always went with Jacobson. But in 1910 the schooners quit sealing, then the government closed the seal hunt. We were told that we no longer were allowed to hunt fur seals. To do so would be to break the white man's law. It was a very bad time. We had become so dependent on working for the white hunters that we now had no money to buy food from the traders' stores, and the seals were almost all gone. Some fur seals we could still see in our territory, but we were told that we could not kill them, even to feed our families. We were now poor. We had never been poor before because the fur seal supplied our food and clothing and balance was maintained. We were now frightened to voice our concerns. We received no compensation."

Epilogue
The Heart
of the People

Today, the Huu-ay-aht work to preserve their traditional territories. Over the decades since the outsiders arrived and changed their world, great harm has come to the environment, and to the Huu-ay-aht themselves, who were almost obliterated because of disease. Their culture and traditional knowledge were nearly lost. Gradually, the Huu-ay-aht have grown, and many have left the territory, moved away from the small Indian Reservations defined in the late 19th century. But they have recently taken bold steps to control their future. The language is now taught in their schools, the knowledge of the elders is preserved by modern means of audiotape, videotape, and CDs, and a new pride in their heritage has changed the way they interact with their neighbours.

One important project symbolizing this rebirth is an ambitious scheme to halt the ecological destruction of the land. Logging and fishing during the 1940s and 1950s took much from the land and the ocean, and did not give anything back. Clear-cut logging allowed the hillsides to erode, took away wildlife, and damaged salmon streams. Unregulated commercial fishing reduced the numbers of salmon and other fish stocks. The Huu-ay-aht could no longer live off the land, as had been their traditional way. Losing this intimate connection to the land contributed to the loss of their own cultural understanding. Each generation became more distantly removed from understanding in their hearts the world view expressed by Chief Louie, that "all is one."

To return their people to greatness, the Huu-ay-aht understand that their land must first be healed. They have organized partnerships with government and industry to restore the Sarita River as a major salmon-bearing river. This will be a costly project, and a lengthy one. It will take much time and money, but even more so, it will take great faith and personal commitment from everyone.

To afford the Sarita restoration, the Huu-ay-aht needed to find the financing. The only way to obtain financing involved an extremely emotional decision, but one which in the larger view seemed entirely appropriate. The Huu-ay-aht determined that they would have to use their sacred wood. By selectively logging some of the great red cedars, those trees so integral to their traditional lives, money was raised to help bring back the river, to reclaim it for all. The Sarita is now being restored, and once again some salmon run up it each autumn to spawn. Soon, the Huu-ay-aht believe, it will once more be abundant. The Sarita is the "heart of the people." It is the largest of the 35 rivers and streams in their traditional territories, and is the first to be healed. This river, and the Huu-ay-ahts' success in starting to heal it, mark a new chapter in their long history. Now the Huu-ay-aht show the way for other First Nations, and provide a model for the future.

Place Names Glossary

For the ease of most readers, place names and other Native words in the accounts are rendered in an approximate spelling in English of how these words sound in the language of the Huu-ay-aht. For accuracy, these words and names are presented in this glossary in their Native linguistic transcription. The currently used "common" place names are also provided, where such usage exists.

Place Names Glossary

English	Linguistic	"Common" Name
Anacla	ʔaanaqƛa	Anacla
Cha'pis	čapʔis	Dodgers Cove
Ch'ima'tokosoa	čimataqsuʔa	Cape Beale
Clutus	ƛuutʼas	Clutus
Malsit	maƛsit	Malsit
Kaka'apiya	kakaʼpiya	
Keeha	kiixaa	Keeha
Kee'hin	kii:xin	Keeshan
Keekee'hinkook	kikiixʔinƙuk	
Mugh-yuu	muuqḥyʼuu	Broughton Peaks
N'aqowis	naquwis	
Nanaskiyis	nanaskiyis	Brady's Beach
Numukamis	nuumaqimyis	Numukamis, Sarita
Ots'o'a	ʔučuʔua	
O'quatsqa	ʔo:ʔquatsqa	
Tl'itsnit	ƛʼitsnit	
Wihata	wiḥaaƚaʔa	
Yashitko'a	yašitquua	Coleman Creek

Bibliography

Arima, Eugene et al. *Between Ports Alberni and Renfrew: Notes on West Coast Peoples.* Canadian Museum of Civilization, 1991.

Arima, Eugene, editor. *The Whaling Indians, West Coast Legends and Stories: tales of extraordinary experience.* Canadian Museum of Civilization, 2000.

Arima, Eugene. *The West Coast (Nootka) People.* British Columbia Provincial Museum, 1983.

Harris, Cole. *Making Native Space: Colonialism, Resistance, and Reserves in British Columbia.* UBC Press, 2002.

Huu-ay-aht First Nations. "Kiix?in Agenda Paper", in Alan L. Hoover, editor. *Nuu-chah-nulth Voices, Histories, Objects & Journeys.* Royal B.C. Museum, 2000.

McMillan, Alan D. *Since the Time of the Transformers: The Ancient Heritage of the Nuu-chah-nulth, Dididaht, and Makah.* UBC Press, 1999.

Scott, R. Bruce. *Bamfield Years: Recollections.* Sono Nis Press, 1986.

Scott, R. Bruce. *Barkley Sound, a history of the Pacific Rim National Park Area.* Sono Nis Press, 1972.

Unpublished or archival records

Blenkinsop, George. Reports submitted to the Department of Indian Affairs, 1874. Ottawa, RG 10. National Archives of Canada.

Carmichael, Alfred. Field Notes Relating to Kee-hin, nd. British Columbia Archives.

Dennis, Robert J. "Chief Louie Nookmiis – First Draft Translation of his Oral History." prepared for Huu-ay-aht First Nation, 1998.

Inglis, Richard L, and James C. Haggarty. *Pacific Rim National Park Ethnographic History*, unpublished, 1986.

O'Reilly, Peter. Diary 1882. British Columbia Archives.

Royal Commission on Indian Affairs for the Province of British Columbia, Transcripts of Testimony, 1914. British Columbia Archives.

Sapir, Edward. Nootka Material, Franz Boaz Collection. American Philosophical Society Library.

Acknowledgments

First and foremost I acknowledge the Huu-ay-aht elders whose sense of purpose in recounting the histories and preserving traditional knowledge has ensured continuity for their people. In particular, Chief Louie Nookmiis was pivotal in bridging the generations. He was born and grew up in a transitional time, and understood his importance as a link between generations before and after.

Thanks is also offered to Huu-ay-aht chiefs and council for their support of this project, in particular, Chief Tliishin Spencer Peters and Robert Dennis Sr.

About the Author

Kathryn Bridge is an archivist and historian who lives in Victoria. She has written several books about pioneers in British Columbia, including *By Snowshoe, Buckboard and Steamer: Women of the Frontier* (winner of the Lieutenant Governor's Medal for Historical Writing) and *Phyllis Munday: Mountaineer* (a finalist at the Banff Mountain Book Festival, and runner-up for the Van City Book Prize). She and her family have explored, camped, and boated in the coastal areas of Vancouver Island over the years.

Photo Credits

Cover: Courtesy of the Royal British Columbia Museum, Victoria, B.C. (PN11465); British Columbia Archives: page 57 (i-61566); Huu-ay-aht First Nation: page 17; Lori Graves: page 37; Royal British Columbia Museum: page 30 (PN 16345), page 40 (PN 4659), page 89 (PN6528-D).

AMAZING STORIES™

TALES FROM THE WEST COAST

Smugglers, Sea Monsters, and Other Stories

HISTORY/ADVENTURE
by Adrienne Mason

Tales from the West Coast
ISBN 1-55153-986-1

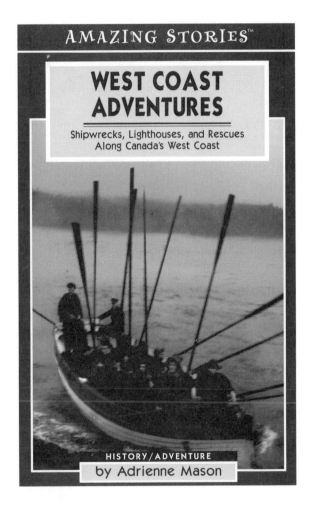

West Coast Adventures
ISBN 1-55153-990-X

AMAZING STORIES™

BRITISH COLUMBIA MURDERS

Mysteries, Crimes, and Scandals

CRIME/MYSTERY
by Susan McNicoll

British Columbia Murders
ISBN 1-55153-963-2

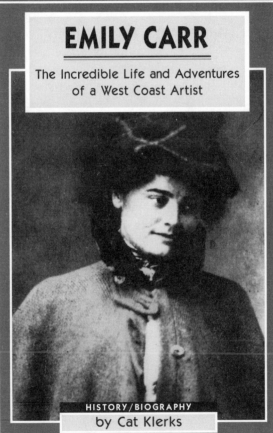

AMAZING STORIES™

EMILY CARR

The Incredible Life and Adventures
of a West Coast Artist

HISTORY/BIOGRAPHY
by Cat Klerks

Emily Carr
ISBN 1-55153-996-9

Ghost Town Stories III
ISBN 1-55153-984-5

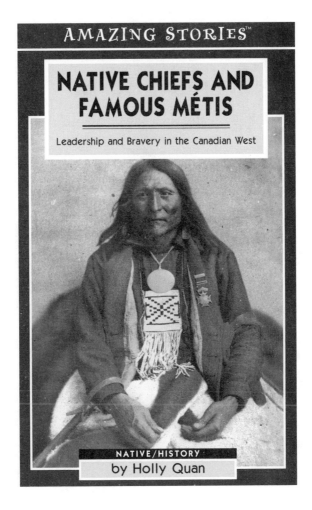

AMAZING STORIES™

NATIVE CHIEFS AND FAMOUS MÉTIS

Leadership and Bravery in the Canadian West

NATIVE/HISTORY
by Holly Quan

Native Chiefs and Famous Métis
ISBN 1-55153-965-9

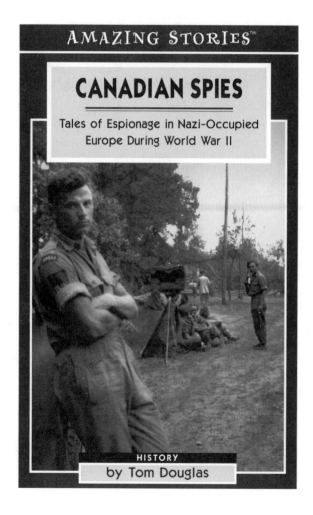

AMAZING STORIES™

CANADIAN SPIES

Tales of Espionage in Nazi-Occupied
Europe During World War II

HISTORY
by Tom Douglas

Canadian Spies
ISBN 1-55153-966-7

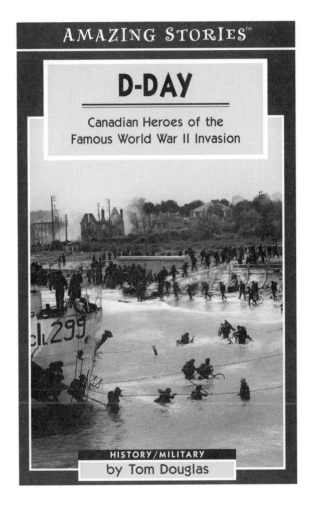

AMAZING STORIES™

D-DAY

Canadian Heroes of the
Famous World War II Invasion

HISTORY/MILITARY
by Tom Douglas

D-Day
ISBN 1-55153-795-8